Tony Leon served for twenty years (1989–2009) as a member of parliament in South Africa and for thirteen years as leader of the Democratic Party and Democratic Alliance, the country's official opposition party. His party leadership commenced in May 1994, within days of Nelson Mandela's inauguration as president. Leon also played a key role in the constitutional negotiations that led to the birth of a democratic South Africa. A lawyer and attorney, he lectured in Constitutional Law at the University of the Witwatersrand, Johannesburg, and served on the Johannesburg City Council before entering parliament.

After standing down from party leadership in 2007, he was awarded a Fellowship to the Institute of Politics, John F Kennedy School of Government, Harvard University, and in 2008 was Visiting Fellow, Cato Institute, Washington DC. In 2009, President Jacob Zuma appointed him as South African ambassador to Argentina, Uruguay and Paraguay, where he served as Head of Mission in Buenos Aires until October 2012.

OPPOSITE MANDELA

Tony Leon

ENCOUNTERS WITH SOUTH AFRICA'S ICON

JONATHAN BALL PUBLISHERS

JOHANNESBURG AND CAPE TOWN

For Peter, a full participant in the period chronicled
in these pages, and for Noa and Etai, and the next generation,
who will live in freedom because of its legacy

ACKNOWLEDGEMENTS

I am grateful to Jonathan Ball the founding and moving spirit of Jonathan Ball Publishers, for conceiving this book and enthusing on its progress from idea to manuscript. Jeremy Boraine, Publishing Director, provided both a professional eye and expert follow-up through to production and then publication. Michael Morris was a careful, thoughtful and efficient editor, whose deft touch and assistance with research improved the text. Lesley Hay-Whitton did the final edits with equal measures of keen-eyed excellence and good humour. My profound thanks to Jan-Jan Joubert, one of the country's best political journalists, for volunteering to do the final fact-checking with his customary diligence. The design was undertaken by Michiel Both (cover) and Kevin Shenton of Triple M Design, and the picture research by Rhianne van der Linde.

Irritatingly, all the mistakes that might appear remain my own.

TONY LEON

CAPE TOWN – JANUARY 2014

Originally published in South Africa in 2014 by
JONATHAN BALL PUBLISHERS (PTY) LTD
A division of Media24 Limited
PO Box 33977
Jeppestown
2043

ISBN 978-1-86842-601-0
ebook ISBN 978-1-86842-602-7

Grateful acknowledgement is made for permission to reprint the following
previously published material:
Excerpts from *Mandela – The Authorised Biography* by Anthony Sampson.
Published by HarperCollins in 1999.
Excerpts from *Mandela – A Biography* by Martin Meredith. Originally published by the
UK Penguin Group in 1997, second edition published by Simon & Schuster/Jonathan Ball in 2010.
Excerpts from *The State of Africa – A History of Fifty Years of Independence* by Martin Meredith.
Published by Jonathan Ball in 2005.
Excerpt from *South Africa's Brave New World – The Beloved Country Since the End of Apartheid* by
RW Johnson. Published by Allen Lane in 2009.
Excerpt from 'Die Kind' by Ingrid Jonker, with permission from The Ingrid Jonker Trust.

Every effort has been made to trace the copyright holders and to obtain their permission
for the use of copyright material. The publishers apologise for any errors or omissions
and would be grateful to be notified of any corrections that should be incorporated
in future editions of this book.

Twitter: http://www.twitter.com/JonathanBallPub
Facebook: http://www.facebook.com/pages/Jonathan-Ball-Publishers/298034457992
Blog: http://jonathanball.bookslive.co.za/

Cover by Michiel Botha
Front cover photograph © Government Communication and Information System (GCIS)
Design and typesetting by Triple M Design, Johannesburg
Back cover photograph © Gallo Images/Beeld/Halden Krog
Printed and bound by Paarl Media, Paarl
Set in 11,5/18 pt Adobe Garamond Pro

CONTENTS

'It was not the Roman army which conquered Gaul, but Caesar;
it was not the Carthaginian army which caused the Republican army
to tremble at the gates of Rome, but Hannibal;
it was not the Macedonian army which reached the Indus, but Alexander.'
— EMPEROR NAPOLEON BONAPARTE

Introduction

JOHANNESBURG'S MILPARK HOSPITAL, in the suburb of Parktown West, was an unlikely place in early December 1998 for an encounter between the president of South Africa and one of his political opponents.

Fate, a bad genetic inheritance and some dissolute habits found me in one of Milpark's private wards on the eve of a quadruple coronary bypass operation. My cardiologist had assured me that any further delay in the operation would mean that my imminent forty-second birthday might well be the last I celebrated.

I had not allowed the timing of the operation to interfere with a hectic political schedule and, in the days preceding my admission to the cardiothoracic section of the hospital, had undertaken a fairly gruelling tour of South Africa's major cities, featuring as the star in showbiz-style rallies in what the Democratic Party, which I had been leading since 1994, billed the 'Leader of the Opposition Tour'. This was something of a stretch: at the time, my party had only seven seats in parliament – out of 400 – nearly seventy fewer than those gained in the 1994 election by the principal opposition formation and previous government, the National Party (NP).

However, my party had, in the preceding four years, made most of the running on the opposition side in parliament, and the polls and a string of by-election victories in previous National Party strongholds suggested that there would be a reversal of fortune for both the NP and my party in the next general election, due six months hence. My political strategists had decided we needed to make the claim for chief opposition status well before election day, hence the 'Leader of the Opposition Tour', which combined razzmatazz with chutzpah. Fortunately, the next election saw the Democratic Party eclipse the once-mighty NP and increase its very modest 1994 tally by over sixfold, confirming our brazenness.

It was during one or other of the city hall rallies a few weeks earlier that, in my usual no-holds-barred style, I had lashed out at the African National Congress cabinet led by Nelson Mandela for what I, along with my supporters, viewed as its lapses of governance. This particular attack clearly angered the president. A day or two afterwards he ridiculed my party – and the increasingly hapless National Party, then languishing under a deeply unpopular leader, Marthinus van Schalkwyk, who had succeeded the consequential former president FW de Klerk in the post – dismissing us both as 'Mickey Mouse parties'. At the next rally, a newspaper reporter asked for my response to the president's attack. Stumped for a meaningful rejoinder, I decided to repay him with a coin from the currency of Walt Disney. 'Well, if I lead a Mickey Mouse party,' I said, 'then Mandela must lead a Goofy government.'

I thought little further of this offhand, and doubtless kindergarten, response. But it clearly delighted the headline writer of *The Citizen* newspaper of Johannesburg; it was splashed on the front page under the banner 'Leon attacks "Goofy government"'.

However, the night before my major heart surgery, both the remark and its target were the furthest things from my mind as I lay in bed anxiously awaiting my fate, in the company of my Israeli girlfriend, and soon-to-be wife, Michal. At around 5pm, there was a knock on the door and a world-famous voice, by now very familiar to me, called out from the other side, 'Hello, Mickey Mouse, this is Goofy. Can I come in?'

It was indeed Nelson Mandela. He entered the room alone, beaming a smile at us and radiating his customary charm. He wished me well for the next day's procedure, chatted for a few moments and then left. It was a good augury for the operation, which was successfully concluded.

In that now-fading memory snapshot, this visit characterised the essence of Mandela and the relationship he forged with the political figures of his time, and a throng of humanity beyond the confines of government and party politics.

My perspective of Mandela and his presidency provides a different vantage point from that of many others – from the parliamentary opposition, which was, paradoxically, both distant from and close to his presidency. The pages that follow in this memoir reflect this view. Throughout the Mandela presidency (1994–1999) I led a small parliamentary party in opposition to the mighty behemoth he bestrode. My political and parliamentary leadership, which commenced just a few days after his inauguration as president, in May 1994, was, initially, concerned with re-establishing relevance after a crushing electoral defeat.

He, in contrast, assumed office after a sweeping and historic victory, propelled in no small measure by his heroic struggle and sacrifice. He was an authentic global celebrity, arguably the most admired figure of his age. I was tasked with the problem of strategising the survival of my political movement. He was burdened with much greater things: binding the wounds of a divided nation and reconciling the divided communities he now led, which had, almost until the day he swore allegiance to a constitution enacted just months before, been in a state of conflict with one another, much of it violent. That South Africa stood much taller after his storied five-year presidency, and was so much more at peace with itself and the world, having secured its democratic and constitutional foundations on once-fragile ground, owed much to this singular man.

I have always wrestled in relation to my encounters with Mandela – and other leaders I met personally or viewed through the lens of history – with the difficulty of separating the power of human agency from what Karl Marx termed the 'motive forces of history', or the confluence of events and the formations that propelled them. Undoubtedly, while Mandela was at all times the servant and symbol of the political movement he came to lead, he also at key moments provided personal leadership that proved quite decisive in determining the course of this country.

Of the personal, Mark Twain reminds us, '[e]very man is a moon with a dark side that he doesn't show anyone'. We can also bracket Mandela with Mahatma Gandhi as one of the select few of any era who transcend the politics of their age and rank in that rare category of the truly good and great. But we should bear in mind George Orwell's necessary caution and apply it to both men: 'The problem with conferring sainthood on Gandhi is that you need to rescue saints from under a pile of tissues and saccharine.'

Some parts of this book reflect encounters, private and public, that display the blind spots that sometimes occluded the otherwise hopeful and positive vision of a harmonious and multiracial South Africa promised by Mandela's presidency, and his life of struggle and imprisonment before it. But that, again, only paints him as human and not as a deity, as some of his more gushing but misguided admirers have sought to portray him.

From the perspective of 2014, I still believe – perhaps more emphatically today than when I delivered it – that my tribute to his achievement when parliament took leave of him in March 1999 holds true:

> I am deeply honoured that I have been able to see from these benches the ending of apartheid and the beginning of democracy under the presidency of Nelson Mandela. My respect and admiration for him is unconditional. He graces this House. He graces this country. He graces humanity.

On a more personal note, I wrote in my subsequent 2008 autobiography *On the Contrary – Leading the Opposition in a Democratic South Africa,* which I have liberally consulted (along with diary notes and other sources) in writing this volume: 'Mandela was an extraordinary phenomenon. At one level he was all too human, but at another level he inhabited a plane out of reach of most mortal politicians.'[1] I place myself very much in the latter category.

Certainly, as I experienced it from up close, the Mandela presidency was an all-inclusive effort, which operated on many fronts. He led a Government of National Unity until 1996, and, no sooner had its largest minority component (the National Party) left it than he sought to include others, not least my party, in it. This extraordinary proposition, had I accepted it, would likely have altered the course of the current opposition trajectory in South Africa. But, as the pages that follow reflect, we could not agree to square the circle of being both in opposition and in government.

Throughout the Mandela presidency and for some years before it, I was often at the receiving end of what the ghostwriter of his autobiography, and, latterly, managing editor of *Time* magazine, Richard Stengel called 'The Full Mandela'. He defined it well:

> He is a power charmer – confident that he will charm you, by whatever means possible. He is attentive, courtly, winning, and, to use a word he would hate, seductive ... The charm is political as well as personal ... and he regards himself not so much as the Great Communicator but as the Great Persuader ... He would always rather persuade you to do something than order you to do so ... [But he] will always stand up for what he believes is right with a stubbornness that is virtually unbending.[2]

I used to tell my political colleagues after one or another session with the great man and a dose of 'The Full Mandela' that, from an opposition perspective, it was a little like *Fatal Attraction*. And Stengel provides us with another clue to the modus operandi of the 'Great Persuader':

> His charm is in inverse proportion to how well he knows you. He is warm with strangers and cool with intimates. That warm benign

smile is bestowed on every new person who comes within his orbit. But the smile is reserved for outsiders.[3]

The extraordinary range of impulses – sometimes embracing and warm, and at other times distant and hostile – that Mandela deployed in his relationships with his democratic opponents is fully investigated in these pages.

Mandela had, famously, special relationships with a vast array of people, from the famous and powerful to the obscure and humble. In the former category fell Queen Elizabeth II, who once said of her own self-described *annus horribilis* that 'distance is well known to lend enchantment'. She was describing the year 1992 when marital scandals afflicted two of her sons and her home at Windsor Castle caught fire.

In contrast, the years of Mandela's presidency constituted a sort of national and personal *anni mirabiles,* or years of wonder. It could be said that, today, his country (and my own), viewed against the weak leadership, corruption scandals, misgovernance and intensely frayed communal relations, is enduring its own *annus horribilis,* or indeed has suffered a succession of them.

But, a caution: his great personal characteristics aside, Mandela's presidency had the advantage of occurring at a time of transcending national and international change. He was the book end between the dying of the old order and the dawn of a new age. By the time he took office, the fifty-year era of Communist rule over Eastern Europe, and forty-six years of apartheid rule (and three centuries of racial domination) at home, had just come to at an end. It was an era of new, brave and dramatic beginnings.

It was on his watch that a new constitution was negotiated and inked, the Truth and Reconciliation Commission commenced and concluded its work, and the country and its first citizen basked in the attention and admiration of the world. Such an alignment of stars is rare in any country's history. It is equally true that sometimes it is easier to guide the ship of state through the high seas of big events than it is to navigate the shallower, but often swifter and more treacherous, currents through which it fell to his successors to manoeuvre.

But, some gaffes and errors aside, which I also examine in this book, Mandela led by example in opening up the free space necessary for a democracy to take root in this country. His rare combination of personal history and the enforced twenty-seven-year period of reflection and introspection perhaps uniquely equipped him for the task of being the country's cheerleader-in-chief for democratic freedom.

When Mandela was gravely ill in hospital in August 2013, his close colleague Pallo Jordan reminded us: 'During the Rivonia trial [at which he defended himself against the High Treason charges, which could have resulted in his execution], Nelson Mandela cited the Magna Carta, the Petition of Rights, and the US Bill of Rights as expressive of his vision of a free society.'[4]

No less than his own movement's Freedom Charter, these international testaments of freedom clearly informed and helped shape his world view and his tone of governance.

Equally, Mandela's rich and complex background helped inform and shape the powerful and symbolic gestures that so marked his presidency and defined his leadership style.

British statesman Lord Denis Healey once said properly rounded leaders needed 'a hinterland', a life and philosophy beyond the narrow confines of the party *Diktate*. Few of any country's rulers – and certainly none here since his presidency – have enjoyed Mandela's breadth of experience. Although this book makes no claim to being a full, or even partial, biography of the man, the encounters I had with him, and the events of his later years that I witnessed, were testimony to his extraordinary roundness both as a person and as a politician.

Richard Stengel, again, captures the complex and contradictory forces that shaped his life and informed his politics: 'His persona is a mixture of African royalty and British aristocracy. He is a Victorian gentleman in a silk dashiki.'[5]

Politics and imprisonment might have shaped his life, but so too did his decision to escape an early arranged marriage, commence the first black law practice in Johannesburg, and earn a living independent of the party. He was more certifiable member of the human race than narrowly formed political partisan.

Doubtless it was this rich personal hinterland that allowed him to call the queen of England by her first name, and to win the adulation of rural peasants in his home province. It also informed some of his most powerful gestures and symbols.

Today, in contrast, almost our entire political leadership is drawn from the ranks of lifetime politicians and trade unionists. This is not confined to the governing party; many emerging leaders on the opposition side, as well, have had no career outside party politics.

Gestures and symbols are hugely important, and often underestimated, in statecraft, and Mandela had an almost genius-like ability to use them to shape his nation and bind its component parts together, as the chapters that follow reflect.

He set the benchmark even before entering office, at a dramatic moment on the eve of South Africa's first democratic election in 1994. Towards the end of the only television debate between him and President FW de Klerk – in the main, a rancorous and point-scoring exercise, with the ANC leader spending much of it on the offensive – Mandela reached across to De Klerk, took his hand and said of his main rival, 'I am proud to hold your hand ... Let us work together to end division and suspicion.' Posterity remembers that gesture better than the debate, and thus the 'Rainbow Nation' was born.

Paradoxically, Mandela, the most partisan of politicians, was also able to look beyond the interests of the party and make tough calls on it to meet the needs of the country-in-the-making.

There was another critical moment just after the 1994 elections, during its chaotic counting process. Today South Africa's first democratic election is remembered in reverential terms, even tinged with a touch of the miraculous. For those of us involved in it, and even for others who can remember its detail, it was a far more jagged affair, with its mess of unreconciled ballots, pirate voting stations and other jarring irregularities. During the long tallying process, the very future hung in the balance due to extreme electoral infringements in key places. At one point, senior ANC officials met in Johannesburg and demanded the party take action, and at least call a press conference, concerning what many insiders apparently regarded as 'grand theft', which they believed had robbed the party of victory in KwaZulu-Natal and elsewhere. An eyewitness at the meeting describes its conclusion:

> Mandela had said nothing during the discussion. Then he brought the
> room to a full stop. 'Tell the comrades to cancel the press conference.

We will not do anything to make the election illegitimate. The ANC will not say the election is not "free and fair". Prepare our people in Natal and the Western Cape to lose.[6]

He followed through on this example when, towards the end of his presidency, the Truth and Reconciliation Commission prepared to publish its interim report in October 1998, and both his predecessor and successor as president attempted legal action either to amend or to suppress its findings. In contrast, Mandela said the equivalent of 'publish and be damned'. As his authorised biographer, Anthony Sampson, noted: 'As head of state he saw himself as having loyalties which went beyond the ANC ...'[7]

Indeed, as president and even before, Mandela ensured that his presidential office was no echo chamber reserved only for approving voices. He sought the counsel of a range of viewpoints.

While he was unyielding on his bottom lines, Mandela claimed no monopoly of wisdom on key issues and sought a range of views and voices beyond the party faithful and his inner circle. Perhaps that is precisely the reason why, as someone so outside the circle of his movement, I enjoyed such access to him and he, mostly, seemed to relish an outsider perspective.

A different set of attitudes prevails today in South Africa's inner councils of power. A gloomy, but, I fear, accurate, description of it appeared in an editorial in the local *Financial Mail* in August 2013:

Rightly or wrongly, the ANC struggles to bring itself to listen to any institution, organisation or individual outside its own ranks. The most important debates within the ANC happen within the ANC. In the minds of the cadres, many of whom think of themselves as part of a liberation movement rather than a political party, outside critiques are almost by definition wrong.[8]

I know, from the leadership position that I occupied for thirteen years in parliament, that contrary voices are often irritating and discomforting. But they are vital for obtaining society's buy-in and correcting course when change is indicated. They are often the equivalent of the canary in the coal mine, giving early warning of dangers that lie ahead.

At our first meeting after the 1994 election, Mandela told me, 'It is important for the opposition to hold up a mirror to the government and point out where we do things wrong.' He used almost exactly the same formula when, in public, he benchmarked his soon-to-be-elected government's relationship with the media. In February 1994, Mandela told the International Press Institute Congress:

> … the media are a mirror through which we can see ourselves as others perceive us, warts, blemishes and all. The African National Congress has nothing to fear from criticism. I can promise you, we will not wilt under close scrutiny. It is our considered view that such criticism can only help us grow, by calling attention to those of our actions and omissions which do not measure up to our people's expectations and the democratic values to which we subscribe.[9]

Four years in office changed Mandela's views, both on opposition and on media scrutiny. In December 1997, at the ANC's 50th conference in Mafikeng (since renamed as Mahikeng), he severely criticised the press, non-governmental organisations, the opposition and other elements of civil society. He identified them as part of some vast and ill-defined 'counter-revolutionary movement'.

However intemperate those remarks, they are a far cry from the poisoned waters that seem to separate government and the media, the opposition and civil society today. They certainly did not lead to the introduction of any legislation to muzzle the media, such as South Africa has witnessed in more recent times. But perhaps it sowed the seeds for a future showdown.

As I commenced writing this book in mid-2013 and Mandela lay gravely ill in hospital in Pretoria, a fierce contest was being waged about his legacy. On one hand, the ruling African National Congress – of which he was a devoted member – certainly embraced Nelson Mandela and his early record of armed struggle and revolutionary leadership, and revelled in the reflected glory of his past leadership. But it was far more ambivalent about what I have termed 'latter Mandelaism', or Mandela's mostly staunch fealty to the constitution, his respect for its institutions and his acceptance of judicial processes, even those that found against him. Most of all, it had placed itself at a vast remove from the non-racial Rainbow Nation that arguably was the leitmotiv of the Mandela presidency. Mandela died, mourned by the world, on 5 December 2013; I elaborate, in the final chapter, on how far or distant we are from his legacy, and what clues our current situation offers to South Africa's future.

But the behaviour of those on the other side of the political fence, by contrast, was no less partial and incomplete. The principal opposition party, which I had led for thirteen years, the Democratic Alliance (DA)[10] was determined, also somewhat clumsily, to lay claim to the Mandela legacy. In 2013 it began a propaganda exercise under the title 'Know your DA', in which photographs of Mandela with Progressive Party (a predecessor movement) stalwart Helen Suzman accompanied text that neatly suggested that the opposition's roots lay in the same struggle as Mandela's, and that it was the rightful heir to his vision of a non-racial constitutional democracy. The leapfrogging and eliding of narrative provided by this partial history (which obliterated my own leadership and ignored entirely the fact that the party had staunchly opposed both the armed struggle and the campaign of economic disinvestment from the apartheid state, two totems Mandela strongly embraced) caused me some wry amusement as well as irritation, and provoked anger in others. But, like the ANC's claims, it failed to capture either the complete picture or the man it venerated in full.

I wrote this book with neither airbrush nor agenda, but rather a desire to record highlights of the extraordinary seventeen years from Mandela's release from prison in early 1990 to our last encounter when I announced my retirement from party leadership in November 2006. I do so in the hope that it provides an interesting and unusual, and mostly a first-hand, perspective on one of the most extraordinary leadership figures of our time and indeed on the most dramatic and remarkable years of my country's history-in-the-making thus far.

CHAPTER ONE

Release

WHEN I TOOK my backbench seat on 2 February 1990, the first-sitting day of a parliament to which I had been elected for the first time some five months earlier, South Africa was on the brink of transcendent change. Quite how transcendent it would be was about to be revealed in the opening speech of the newly elected president, FW de Klerk. Unbeknown to me then, I would sit through nearly twenty more such presidential addresses in the future. None had the thermonuclear intensity of De Klerk's announcements that Friday morning in the national legislature in Cape Town; indeed, its after-effects are still being felt today.

In the 1989 election, De Klerk's ruling National Party (NP), to whose leadership he had been elected earlier that year after his strongman predecessor, PW Botha, had been felled by a stroke, polled less than 50 per cent of the total vote. In what was to be the last all-white election (held in parallel with elections to the separate Coloured and Indian chambers), this was its lowest haul of the poll in a generation or more. He had lost ground mostly to the far-right-wing Conservative Party (CP), which obtained around 30 per cent of the votes. The reform-minded, liberal Democratic Party (DP), in whose various iterations I had been involved for much of my then-young life (I joined at age eleven and became an MP at thirty-two), brought up the rear with 21 per cent. However, the delimitation and vagaries of the constituency system allocated the NP a comfortably bigger overall majority in the new parliament than the voting totals suggested.

But De Klerk was not simply hemmed in by his own electorate and his party's declining fortunes within it. On the one hand, the NP held a near monopoly of formal political power, bolstered through its control of the security forces and the doctrine of the supremacy of parliament, which meant even the most independent-minded judges (of whom there were a few) could only on occasion ameliorate, rather than strike down, legislation or executive acts.

On the other hand, however, as legendary US President Lyndon B Johnson once observed, 'power is where power goes', and, by the time the tricameral parliament was summoned to hear its new president, much of the power in South Africa had haemorrhaged from its formal structures. 'People's power' was on the march in cities and townships, galvanised by an increasingly assertive trade union movement and an even larger and loosely led (to avoid government crackdowns) civic formation, the United Democratic Front (UDF), which both gave voice to an increasingly militant and still formally powerless black majority, and acted as a sort of internal *Doppelgänger* for the still-banned African National Congress (ANC).

Outside South Africa, the ANC in exile in Lusaka and elsewhere had become ever more vocal and effective in unleashing a campaign for 'people's power' against both the authorities of the apartheid state and its many internal black allies. It was engaged in an increasingly bloody and vicious fight in my home province of Natal with its major opponent there, the Inkatha movement of Chief Mangosuthu Buthelezi.

I, in common with many others, observed of the internal state of emergency imposed by the government on most urban areas, coupled with a growing international campaign of isolation, sanctions and disinvestment, that South Africa was a country at war with itself and bereft of international allies. This was no exaggeration. The ferment in South Africa was mirrored by the end-of-regime events in Eastern Europe and beyond, where the once-mighty Soviet empire began to crumble and the Berlin Wall had fallen just months before. Freedom was definitely, although unevenly, on the march and its nemesis, tyranny, was in head-long retreat. But where the chips would fall in South Africa remained the key, unanswered, question of the day.

De Klerk had provided some clues in the months between his election the previous September and his debut speech in parliament as president on 2 February that he was going to change the predictable and wearying terms of political trade in South Africa, perhaps best described as hesitant reforms hedged by lashings of repression. He had, for example, already released from life imprisonment nine major ANC leaders, first Govan Mbeki and then eight others, including Walter Sisulu and Ahmed Kathrada. Also, days after the election, he overruled his securocrats and allowed a mass march, led by two of the major internal figures of opposition, the clerics Desmond Tutu and Allan Boesak, to proceed without police interference. He also dismantled the key internal military, and secretive, apparatus, the National Security Management System, established and empowered by his predecessor, PW Botha, who placed great faith in military solutions to primarily political problems.

But it still remained far from clear that De Klerk, whose ascent to power had been marked by his careful cultivation of conservative credentials, would 'go the whole hog' and commence direct negotiations with the major banned black opposition movements, whose most significant component, the ANC, could not operate, or even legally hoist its banner, on home soil. Its key leader, Nelson Mandela, remained in prison, and the question and terms of his release remained the standout issue of the day.

Unknown to those of us outside the walls of state and ANC power, there had been a flurry of secret meetings between high-end government officials and ANC exiled leadership. And Mandela, who had, in December 1988, been transferred after medical treatment from Pollsmoor prison to the relative comfort of a warder's house at Victor Verster prison outside Paarl in the Western Cape winelands, had himself been involved in several years' talks with state officials, led by Justice Minister Kobie Coetsee. He had also, it was later revealed, enjoyed a recent, apparently pleasant, *tête-à-tête* with PW Botha himself, at which the president had poured the tea for his guest, by then the most famous prisoner in the world.

This is a thumbnail sketch of the background canvas on which De Klerk was to paint his outline for his country's future that morning in parliament. Few in the chamber or outside it knew just what bold brushstrokes he would use.

From my perch right at the back of the vast parliamentary chamber, but with a clear view of the podium from where he spoke, I studied the new president closely and recorded my impression of him as he began his game-changing speech:

> De Klerk, superficially, seemed both self-confident and grounded; he bore no chest full of medals; carried no homburg hat; nor did he strut with the overbearing sense of self-importance I had long associated with the leadership of the ruling party. Yet when he stood behind the podium of parliament and in increasingly assertive cadences buried the apartheid way of doing business forever, he seemed immensely elevated and strong.[1]

The speech lasted for not much longer than forty minutes, and with the flourish of a theatrical showman, or seasoned trial lawyer, he saved the most dramatic and far-reaching announcements for the end: a moratorium on the imposition of the death penalty, the acceptance of a negotiated new constitutional order with all leaders and, as a consequence of this, the unconditional release of Nelson Mandela in the very near future – as well as the lifting of all legal and other prohibitions on the ANC, Pan Africanist Congress (PAC), South African Communist Party (SACP), Congress of South African Trade Unions (Cosatu), United Democratic Front (UDF) and allied organisations.

Actually, for all its stupendous impact and the political courage it took to conceive and implement it, the opening line of De Klerk's address contained a half-truth or a white lie, when he proclaimed: 'The general election of 6 September 1989 placed our country irrevocably on the road to drastic change.'[2]

In truth, his election campaign and the mandate he obtained from it were far more ambiguous. Even in my own constituency of Houghton, where he addressed an election meeting (to no avail for his party's candidate who got an electoral thrashing a few days later), De Klerk pilloried my party as guileless satraps of the banned ANC. But, by combining the total votes of the NP and DP in his speech, he co-opted, ex post facto, a mandate for irrevocable change. A former leader of the opposition, Frederik Van Zyl Slabbert, who had imploded his own parliamentary career by resigning from the same chamber just four years earlier, waspishly observed later: 'There is ample and comprehensive evidence that De Klerk's speech on 2 February … was a sell-out of everything the NP had held near and dear since 1948.'

But this noting and protesting (the essence of which the Conservative Party and other elements of the then-strong forces of white right-wing reaction in South Africa were to denounce vehemently, and some even violently reject, in the following years) mattered little. De Klerk had gone where no white leader with power had ventured before. And now the pivot, and the attention of the world, turned towards another, very different, political figure – Nelson Mandela.

To this day, a debate continues on what led De Klerk to dismantle the house of privilege and racial domination he had been bequeathed. He himself later said that he saw 'only disaster if [we] had dug in our heels'.[3] Emboldened by the collapse of Communism, and the lessened fear of its takeover in South Africa, he decided to press ahead. In an interview twenty years later, in 2010, he claimed that his conversion to the politics of negotiation was neither a Damascene epiphany nor a retreat; rather, according to his version, his speech that day was the 'conclusion of a gradual process'.[4] Others suggested that he had little option, and his contribution to history was to have the intelligence to read the proverbial writing on the wall and, in direct contrast to his predecessors, not to assume it was addressed to someone else.

Of all the dramatic announcements that De Klerk made on that day, perhaps the singularly momentous one was the imminent and unconditional release of Mandela. For most of my life – and for all South Africans aged under forty or so – Mandela had been, literally and figuratively, the political equivalent of 'the king across the water' – or the expanse of sea between the Cape Peninsula and the grim Robben Island prison where he had spent nineteen of his twenty-seven years' incarceration. He was, at once, both the most spoken-of and the most distant of the many figures who dominated the political landscape. But dominate from a distance, unseen except by a select few, he certainly did.

In 1964, I was just seven years old, in the second year of primary school in Durban, when Mandela had been sentenced to life imprisonment. Years later, as a student at the left-leaning University of Witwatersrand (appropriately, one of his alma maters) in the 1980s, I had involved myself in the seemingly audacious 'Release Mandela' campaign in which members of the student body went about with petitions demanding the release of the imprisoned icon. It had – like smoking marijuana or furtive sex – elements of the daring and illicit about it, and it proved (or improved) one's radical chic credentials. But of the man in whose name we collected signatures, we could see no picture, nor could we read (legally at least) any of his movement's literature.

Even back then, though, and based on the information that could be gleaned, I decided the socialist and even militant ANC held little appeal, and that it offered few viable solutions to creating the conditions for inclusive economic growth and democratic freedom that South Africa needed. My deep and abiding dislike of the narrow racial nationalism of the regnant National Party did not, unlike so many of my fellow students, lead me to adopt its opposite in the form of the ANC. The middle ground occupied by liberal and reformist movements such as the Progressive Federal Party (precursor to the Democratic Party) might have lacked the outlaw radical dash and glamour of the movements in exile, with their imprisoned leaders. But on its duller, yet, I thought, surer ground I pitched my political tent.

However, whether you were a close ANC camp follower or as distant from his movement as I was, Mandela exercised a magnetic pull on most politically conscious imaginations.

In the nine days between De Klerk's detonating his big bang in parliament and Mandela's designated release date, I joined my country and its people in wondering just who would emerge from the gates of the Victor Verster prison and what he would say. I also knew that, from that moment on, nothing in South Africa would ever be the same.

I subsequently learnt that all manner of arm-wrestling between De Klerk and Mandela had occurred when they met a few days later: where and when he was to be released apparently led to heated disputes between the two leading figures on South Africa's political stage. De Klerk apparently wanted him flown to Johannesburg almost immediately, while Mandela wanted to walk out from his Paarl prison and then address the people of Cape Town. Not for the last time, the prisoner was to prevail over the president.[5]

I was quite shocked when I saw a photograph of the encounter the next day; the body language looked very stiff and strained – not surprising, in view of the tensions later revealed of that encounter between them. Mandela flashed a pro forma smile while De Klerk looked peevish, as though he would rather be anywhere else. But I was more struck by both the gauntness and great age of Mandela, then seventy-one, who was showing some signs of his 10 000 days in jail. Before this, the only photographs in circulation had been taken almost three decades before, and they portrayed a bearded and obviously much younger man with a chubby face. The other noteworthy feature from this historic and uncomfortable photo opportunity was how Mandela physically towered over De Klerk. This physiological fact would, over time, serve as a sort of political metaphor for the years that were to follow.

The meaning of the moment when, two days later, Mandela finally walked out of Victor Verster prison, a free man 're-joining a country which had grown up without him', is vividly captured by his authorised biographer Anthony Sampson:

> Mandela walked out of the prison gates on 11 February, holding hands with [his wife] Winnie. It provided the most powerful image of the time, even in an era of charismatic heroes overcoming tyrannies in Eastern Europe and Russia: of Gorbachev, Walesa, Havel and the fall of the Berlin Wall. For Mandela embodied a more elemental and universal myth, like a revolutionary opera or *The Odyssey*, depicting the triumph of the human spirit, the return of the lost leader. And his long isolation had allowed the myth to take off from the man, leaving everything to the imagination: a dotted line within which anyone could fill in their own detailed picture of a hero.[6]

My elder brother, Peter, was staying with me in Cape Town that day, having, along with my parents, come to parliament to attend my maiden speech a few days before – an event of family pride but of little political consequence in such historic and heady times. We both set off on the day of the release to the Grand Parade in central Cape Town, along with an estimated 50 000 others, to await Nelson Mandela's expected early-afternoon appearance on the balcony of the City Hall. This was my first direct experience of an ANC event, and it was not auspicious.

The crowds in front pushed backwards and those behind pushed forwards. The middle ranks, where I was standing (perhaps an appropriate metaphor for the political ground my party occupied), were being squeezed out. When the delay mounted and the crowd's irritation grew to unrest and some looting broke out on the fringes, the police, who ringed the crowd, opened fire with birdshot. Cape Town journalist Michael Morris described the scene well:

> With every cracking shot, the crowd lurched en masse, unsteadied briefly. Some flinched but nobody ran. The tinny clanking of countless empty cooldrink tins underfoot matched the fidgety surges of the shoulder-to-shoulder mass, but it was an immovable body. Nobody would be deflected from the event of the century, as many saw it, the uncanny reappearance of Nelson Mandela.[7]

In fact Peter and I were not as staunch as most in the massed crowd and decided to retreat home after about an hour and a half of waiting for the much-delayed arrival of Mandela. To my amazement, when I presented myself some four hours later at an ambassador's residence for a cocktail function, I discovered that the world's most famous political prisoner had not yet arrived to speak.

In the event (which I watched on a small TV set in an upstairs room of the ambassadorial residence), when he finally appeared, framed by the faded Edwardian splendour of the City Hall balcony after a four-hour delay and before a much-diminished crowd, his was not a great or reassuring message. The script (apparently) was written by a committee and promised lashings of nationalisation of industry and other delights plucked from the then-decidedly depleted cupboard of international socialism.

Mandela's delivery of it was as halting and I thought as unconvincing as the message itself. He spoke of himself as '"a loyal and disciplined" member of the ANC' and promised that the era of negotiations opened by De Klerk 'cannot take place above the heads or behind the backs of our people'. He recommitted himself to armed resistance and called for an intensification of the 'struggle on all fronts'. He made a nod towards De Klerk as 'a man of integrity' and expressed the hope 'that a climate conducive to a negotiated settlement would be created soon' and the armed struggle then suspended.[8]

But these were about the only elements in it that joined the thread he had so powerfully woven in his famed, and arguably life-saving, speech from the criminal dock at the Rivonia Trial some twenty-seven years before. Although he did repeat part of his famous message of inter-racial harmony and democratic uplift ('I have fought against white domination, and I have fought against black domination. I have cherished the ideal of a democratic and free society in which all persons live together in harmony with equal opportunities'), in the main it was an uncompromising message. Doubtless it was reassuring to, and aimed at, his core constituency, but it was of less reassurance to the rest of us. The late poet and essayist Stephen Watson recalled the same day's events in a tone that evoked a moment of disappointment:

> When I had gone to Cape Town's Grand Parade on the day of Mandela's release … it was with the awareness that few human beings had ever been better set up by history to say unforgettable things than this man on this particular day. Yet all he had produced was a string of party-political platitudes …[9]

But I, along with others disappointed by this first glimpse of the great man, was soon to realise that in Mandela's case (like the media in Marshall McLuhan's conception) '[t]he medium is the message'. He was to prove the most powerful and important messenger and medium on South Africa's stage from that day onwards.

The very next day, and not for the last time either, a very different, less partisan, more emollient Mandela appeared on the sprawling lawns of the Bishopscourt residence of Archbishop Desmond Tutu, where Mandela had spent his first night of freedom. He gave such an assured performance to a throng of hundreds of admiring media representatives that he largely obliterated the memory of the previous night. The gospel he offered that day of reconciliation, negotiation and a marked absence of bitterness so enraptured the normally cynical press corps that they burst into applause at the end.[10] A few days later, he returned in triumph to a homecoming rally of almost 100 000 people in Soweto, near Johannesburg.

Over the next two years South Africa was in an interregnum – 'the old is dying, the new cannot be born' – as the exiting power and the incoming one, the NP and the ANC, set about getting to know each other and establishing conditions for full-throttled negotiations to commence. Most other parties, and certainly my own, were reduced to the role of interested onlookers. We were available to produce a proposal here or a strategy there, and were certainly necessary to provide an illusion of inclusivity.

The process of constitutional negotiations finally got under way in December 1991, nearly two years after the release of Mandela, in the jerry-built and pretentiously named World Trade Centre near the Jan Smuts International Airport on Johannesburg's East Rand. But ANC negotiations supremo Cyril Ramaphosa spelt out the power reality: '[If] we and the National Party agree, everyone else can get stuffed.'[11]

It is not the purpose of this narrative to summarise the treacherous, violent background of those times, which initially derailed those talks, created a climate of mutual suspicion and then, finally, injected them with a sense of urgency. I fully canvassed these events in my political autobiography *On The Contrary – Leading the Opposition in a Democratic South Africa.*[12] However, it became clear early on that this duopoly of NP–ANC decision-making, coupled with their effective exclusion from its circle of influence, greatly angered the Inkatha Freedom Party (IFP) of Mangosuthu Buthelezi.

Ongoing clashes, leading to massacres on occasion, between his supporters and those of the ANC and the hidden or semi-apparent (depending on your viewpoint) hand of the 'third force' of security forces aiding and abetting the IFP attacks, poisoned the well of amity that at first seemed to prevail between the ANC and NP. And then there was the violence of the white right wing, and De Klerk's deep distrust of the ANC due to its prevarications on suspending the armed struggle, and the arrest of some forty of its leaders who, under the code name 'Operation Vula', apparently had a 'plan B' – armed insurrection – in case the talks foundered.

In this gelignite of explosive impulses and forces, it became clear after a by-election in the western Transvaal in February 1992 that the NP had lost its heartland support; this led to De Klerk's audacious gamble a month later, when he called a white referendum and obtained a more than two-thirds support from his electorate to proceed on the path towards a negotiated settlement.

The wind seemed to be behind De Klerk's back until, just three months later, in June, fifty residents of a Vaal Triangle township were killed in a murderous rampage by local Zulu hostel dwellers. Boipatong had lived in the anonymous obscurity of hundreds of other such settlements in the country. But, on that June day, it became a metaphor for all that had gone wrong in the intervening two and a half years since the sun shone so fair as Mandela walked out of prison to freedom.

Although a team of international detectives and the home-grown Goldstone Commission never unambiguously placed the blame for this massacre on the government of the day, Mandela had no doubt about whom to finger for the outrage. 'I can no longer explain to our people,' he fumed, 'why we continue to talk to a regime that is murdering our people.'[13] The on-off talks, at that stage deadlocked over key issues and suspended while mass action by the ANC took hold of the streets, now appeared to many to be dead in the water. But, as with so many illusions and false starts in those momentous times, it might, through the lens of hindsight, have been better described as the 'darkness before dawn'.

Just a month or so after Boipatong had again internationalised the cause and frustrations of the ANC against what it depicted as an untrustworthy government, I received a telephone call. It was Nelson Mandela, and he was inviting me for dinner.

CHAPTER TWO

The Dinner

AFTER A LATE night out in August 1992, before the now-ubiquitous cell phone had arrived in South Africa, I got home to find the red light on my answering machine flashing impatiently. I flipped it to 'play' and was amazed to hear a recording of perhaps the most famous voice in the land. 'Hello, Tony, it's Mandela here,' he intoned with charming informality. 'I'd very much like you and one or two other DP chaps to come round for dinner.'

At that stage, I had served just less than three years in parliament, and, with other members, had been involved in the stop-start constitutional negotiations at the cavernous World Trade Centre, near Johannesburg's international airport. The Boipatong massacre in June had both caused the breakdown of the talks, and led to the UN Security Council's being seized with the matter at a special debate in July.

I happened to be in New York at the time, attending the US Democratic

Party Convention at which the relatively unknown – to the wider world, at least – governor of Arkansas, Bill Clinton, was crowned as nominee for the forthcoming presidential election. I accordingly accompanied a senior MP, Ken Andrew, to the United Nations where he read out our jointly prepared statement on the saga. No one took the slightest notice of our considered contribution, since all eyes that day were on the big political beasts who had flown in from home to address the council: Foreign Minister Pik Botha and ANC President Nelson Mandela.

Botha I knew relatively well from parliament, but I was yet to meet Mandela, although his constant appearances on television and his global status, even then, made him – in the manner of all celebrities – a familiar figure.

This was about to change. That phone call, and my first close-up with 'Madiba', as he became universally known, originated in decidedly local-ised circumstances – as a consequence of his arrival as a resident (then without a vote in view of the racial franchise) in my constituency.

I was an assiduous local MP. Although much engaged in parliamen-tary and constitutional matters at the time, I never forgot the wise advice of legendary US House of Representatives Speaker Tip O'Neill: 'All pol-itics is local'. Also, having the benefits of youthful energy and high levels of political ambition, I never regarded service in the area that had elected me to parliament as a drag or an inconvenience, and spent many hours and days practising the O'Neill dictum in the twenty-two suburbs of north-eastern Johannesburg that comprised the Houghton constituency.

Not every MP in the party shared my enthusiasm. My immediate constituency neighbour in Parktown, party leader Dr Zach de Beer, who was nearly thirty years older than me, once observed in his droll manner, '[t]he voters of Parktown do not bother me, and I certainly don't bother them.'

But Zach and I, and most other MPs, were religious in officiating at the annual ritual of the time, the constituency report-back meeting. This involved hiring a hall, plastering posters and – in those far-off pre-electronic and social media days – sending out pamphlets inviting constituents to attend. Usually, on a good night, around 150 of the 20 000 voters actually did so. But it provided a useful public platform to inform local voters what their representative had been up to – and I never failed to use the event (in carefully prepared press releases sent out in advance) to fire a few missiles at my party's opponents, which in my view very much included the ANC.

As my constituency activists and I were preparing for the August 1992 report-back meeting, a committee member suggested, more I suspect as a gimmick than anything else, that I invite the person who was inarguably now Houghton's most famous resident, Nelson Mandela, to attend. He had recently moved into the area, into a house he later told me was purchased for him by France's President François Mitterrand.

Well, I thought, that's a nice idea, and I hand-wrote an invitation and delivered it together with a chocolate cake to his residence on 13th Avenue a day or two before the meeting. I hardly expected him to avail himself of the invitation, which indeed he did not.

It was when I returned home on the night following the meeting that I had the pleasure of listening to that by-now world-familiar voice on my answering machine. Mandela explained how touched he was by the cake and how pleased he was to have such an energetic representative in parliament, adding, quite unnecessarily I thought, that he was indeed sorry he could not attend the meeting. He was, however, keen to meet, hence his invitation to me 'and one or two other DP chaps' to his house for dinner.

He was as good as his word: a few days later his secretary made arrangements for Ken Andrew, Zach de Beer and me to join him for a meal.

I was intrigued, to put matters mildly, by the invitation. But, as I contemplated the event, I couldn't but reflect why I, aside from my chocolate cake offering, had been asked by Mandela to accompany De Beer and Andrew, far more senior than me in the parliamentary and party hierarchy, and in the unravelling constitutional processes. Perhaps, I surmised, it had something to do with the very voluble stance I had taken in public against the policies and tactics of Mandela's party. I was later to learn that Mandela not only enjoyed a good argument on occasion, but had an almost preternatural talent for reaching out to, and charming, those outside his circle of true believers. If this was the case, then he certainly had my number.

In various public pronouncements, I had raised doubts about the ANC's commitment to liberal democracy and economic freedom, the *raisons d'être* of my party. Some of my DP colleagues were starry-eyed about the party and person of Mandela. I shared their admiration for the man, along with most of the world, but was deeply suspicious of his party and its motives. For example, the previous year – also at a Houghton report-back meeting – I had been less than kind about the ANC, and said of one of its leading thinkers and struggle heroes, Joe Slovo: 'He's an economic illiterate promoting a minimal programme of meaningless populism.'

Aside from my love of the alliterative – and my ignorance of the role that Slovo was in fact playing behind the scenes to steer his party to a more moderate position at the negotiations – there was a real basis for this remark. I had just before that meeting ploughed through Slovo's 100-page polemic 'Has Socialism Failed?' and been aghast at his ex post facto rationalisations of the Communist tyranny, then recently collapsed in the rubble of the Berlin Wall. In the piece, he suggested that Stalin, Mao, Pol Pot and Ceausescu were not the personifications of the entire communist experiment, which had seen tens of millions murdered or starved to death in the course of its implementation, but simply extreme mutants of an otherwise laudable economic and political system.[1]

The argument had not, in fact, really been aimed at its ostensible target, the ANC leadership, but at the more proximate quarry of some fellow DP MPs who were essentially ANC fellow travellers inside our party. It caused a tremendous and predictable fuss with them, but helped crystallise the choice that the party's ever-accommodating leadership, especially the kindly but conflict-averse De Beer, resisted making: on which side of the political divide was the DP positioned? I had little doubt that it was not with the ANC, whose economic and democratic prescriptions were so far removed from our own. Our mutual opposition to apartheid gave us, in my view, little else in common.

However, the speech, and countless other convulsions that racked the party in the months before our dinner with Mandela, had flushed into the open those in our ranks who actually belonged elsewhere. I had been quite relieved when our parliamentary chief whip, Dave Dalling, and four others quit the party and were welcomed into the embrace of the ANC by the ever-beaming Nelson Mandela.

My relief was not only for political positioning reasons, but had a personal element. Dalling's departure left vacant the position of party spokesman on Justice, a high-profile post, especially in fashioning the input for the yet-unwritten constitutional Bill of Rights. De Beer then appointed me as Dalling's replacement. Perhaps Mandela, a consummate student of the intricacies up and down his opponents' hierarchies, had marked this reshuffle.

Whatever the reason for my presence, I looked forward to the encounter. On the appointed evening we presented ourselves, and, after a minimum of security clearance, were ushered into a cosy, but by no means sumptuous, ground-floor living room to await the arrival of the great man. By the standards of the neighbourhood, one of Johannesburg's toniest, the home could have been described as large and comfortable, rather than opulent and ostentatious. It had a reasonably sized garden and the reception rooms, hung with silk drapes, were well appointed. Rather like its now-famous occupant, it was a domestic setting that exuded a stately and decorous elegance.

I had never before met Mandela face-to-face, nor indeed conversed with him, although his ceaseless appearances on TV made him seem somehow very familiar. When he entered the room, casually attired in slacks and T-shirt – adorned with the logo of the Dance Theatre of Harlem, then visiting Johannesburg as the opening act of the recently refurbished Civic Theatre – his famous warmth and conviviality took over and made us, all suited up for the occasion, feel immediately at ease.

I had just returned that day from a lengthy conference in Durban – the so-called British–South Africa meeting – where the political grandees of the UK met with the full range of South African political actors to discourse about the 'way ahead' and related anodyne matters in the climate of suspended constitutional negotiations.

As one of the rapporteurs of the meeting, I had been quoted, in a single paragraph buried deep within the story in that afternoon's edition of *The Star* newspaper. To my amazement, after warmly greeting us, Mandela proceeded to say that, while he understood my perspective, he wanted to explain the ANC's viewpoint. I was smitten! Thus began a relationship that continued and strengthened over the next seventeen years.

Mandela, who was unaccompanied at our get-together, then offered us drinks. Since it was about 7pm, Zach and I (rather than Ken, who was slightly more abstemious) were intensely relieved; but, on eagerly accepting his offer, we were nonplussed when Mandela proceeded to pour us each a glass of port. Out of politeness – since I can't stand the drink – I quaffed mine.

Combining affability with a sense of decorum in almost perfect balance, Mandela continued to put us at ease. When he turned his attention to me, he first asked, 'And how is your father? I remember him well from my days in practice and he sometimes acted for us.'[2] I did not enquire whether this was for his law firm Mandela & Tambo Attorneys, or for the party. But what I found quite revealing from this rather impromptu pleasantry was how politely Mandela elided the far more recent, and high-profile, controversy in which he and my father had been directly involved.

In April, just four months before our dinner together, Mandela and my father had been centre stage in a furious standoff at the University of Natal in Durban. There, my father, by then retired from his long tenure as Supreme Court judge, presided as chancellor, an honorary position of some distinction but whose essential practical task was to confer degrees at graduation ceremonies.

The grand finale of the 1992 week-long graduation events was to be the conferment of an honorary degree on Mandela. However, at a ceremony a few nights earlier, rampaging students protesting about the exclusion of a severely underperforming student, the spectacularly ill-named Knowledge Mdlalose, had carried posters declaring 'Leon is a Murderer'. This, in turn, referred to a controversial death sentence my father had imposed six years before on an ANC bomber, Andrew Zondo, a matter that Mandela and I would discuss at some length several years later.

The ferment on the campus that week placed pressure on three parties: the university's timorous vice-chancellor, Professor James Leatt, Mandela and my father. Following the well-trodden academic path of least resistance, Leatt had urged my father to absent himself from the Saturday graduation ceremony, ostensibly because, as he put it to him, 'Your life might be in danger'. To this entreaty, my father recalled frostily replying, 'Well, let them kill me. I have every intention of being present.'

Mandela was, however, under the greatest pressure of all: his normal decorous sense of *oblige* inclined him to receive the honour from my father, but this ran against the currents unleashed by his own activists, who were determined that their icon should not receive his doctorate from one they termed 'the hanging judge'.

In turn, my father's determination to preside had nothing to do with any bloody-mindedness, but with delivering (as I encouraged him to do) a hard-hitting message about the values that the protesting students and the quiescent administrators were trampling underfoot.

In the event, Mandela withdrew from the ceremony, citing 'reasons of state'. This turn of phrase had an amusing afterlife a few weeks later. The great jurist IA (Isie) Maisels QC, a friend of both Mandela and my father, told me at a dinner arranged by his daughter, Helen Trisk, that 'Mandela couched his excuse in a most curious choice of words since, as of present, he does not yet preside over this or any other state!'

To me, however, it was noteworthy how Mandela's enquiry of my father related to events over four decades earlier, rather than on anything more recent and controversial. But, on other matters, Mandela proved to be far more direct and contemporary.

Before the meal, we asked Mandela about the evolution within the ANC, which was starting to manifest itself in key economic issues. Mandela's response was typical of his candour and directness: 'Well, you know, earlier this year I was a guest at the World Economic Forum in Switzerland, and some of the biggest and most influential businessmen in the world were there. And they were very happy to meet me, but practically every one of them bashed me over the head because of our policy on nationalisation [of industries]. So, when I got back to South Africa, I got hold of our economics team in the ANC, and said to them, "Boys, we are going to have to change our policy in order to be taken seriously in the world." And they agreed ...'

I had no idea whether Mandela's encounter in the Swiss Alps was the decisive factor in the ANC's move away from the socialist model, but I loved the story and the humorous and self-deprecating way Mandela told it. I also thought that, even if much of the World Economic Forum's annual extravaganzas at Davos consisted of pretentious photo opportunities and high-minded junketeering, it had, on this singularly important issue to my country and its future wellbeing, become a sort of modern-day secular Damascus.

Dinner in the adjoining dining room proved to be a pleasant and uncontroversial affair – the meal tasty and unpretentious, accompanied by a sweet white wine that Mandela apparently preferred, though drank little of himself. Notably, he made a point of introducing each of us by name to his domestic worker, a personable courtesy I remember his repeating when he had ascended to the presidency.

Our dinner-table conversation was perhaps noteworthy, again, more for what was *not* discussed than what was actually said. Of the ANC's recently recruited DP MPs, Mandela made no mention. And Zach, certainly, was far too polite to raise the fact that in a sense this meant the bulk of our party, which had declined to join this exodus, saw no essential political meeting point with the party Mandela led. But, of the constitutional negotiations then hanging in the balance, Mandela evinced a fairly optimistic assumption that they would resume at some point in the future – 'once De Klerk has come to his senses', as he phrased it.

Unbeknown to any of us, bar him, a back channel of constant conversations was happening between the chief negotiators of the NP and ANC, Roelf Meyer and Cyril Ramaphosa, which probably explained his statement. In fact, only after another massacre, this time in the Eastern Cape at Bisho (now Bhisho), was a renewed urgency injected into the negotiations, which finally and formally resumed in April the following year.

Since, as we had been alerted in advance, it was Mandela's habit, developed during his decades-long imprisonment, to rise and retire early, proceedings ended at around 9.30pm. He saw us to the door and bade us a very warm farewell, promising 'it will not be long until we see each other again'.

In fact, some twenty months would pass before we did meet formally again, and in even more intimate surrounds, as will be seen in Chapter Three. But by then Mandela and I would occupy very different positions from those we held that night in Houghton. I would no longer be a backbench MP, and he would be president of South Africa. Between those two meetings, South Africa went about dramatically reinventing itself.

Reinvention

A T AROUND 5pm on the evening of 17 November 1993, I was escorted into the makeshift SA Broadcasting Corporation television studio at the World Trade Centre in Kempton Park, where the constitutional negotiations had reached a critical moment. The whole complex, a warren of offices, conference suites and bustling, brightly lit corridors, hummed with a sort of repressed excitement and tension. The studio, with its glare of camera lights and myriad cables snaking across the floor, was all set to beam into the suburbs and townships of a waiting country the news of its next step into a democratic future.

I was quite enjoying my 'fifteen minutes of fame', although the issue that had propelled me into the frontline of this process was far more important than any evanescent esteem it would confer on me or the somewhat sagging fortunes of my party. We were in the final stages of thrashing out a compromise on the crunch question of who would appoint the Constitutional Court judges who would test and interpret South Africa's new constitution. This was one of the key issues that had yet to be agreed in the hours remaining before the overall document was finalised by the waiting delegates.

For all the import of this juncture, the historic moment we had reached as a country, the atmosphere was less one of high expectation and excitement than one of almost subdued weariness. The delegates, including me, had been sapped by the frenetic nature of the last days of the negotiations, and, over the longer haul, the disruptive on-again, off-again nature of the engagement, which had been a feature of the process since it began nearly two years before that fateful, final night. We had been locked in intensive discussion for the best part of five days, both at the World Trade Centre and in the television studios in Johannesburg, where I participated in an ill-tempered debate with NP Minister of Justice Kobie Coetsee.

On the previous weekend, the talks having adjourned until Monday, my party leader, Zach de Beer, had worked the phones with both Mandela and De Klerk to search for a compromise on this key issue, on which I led the Democratic Party push-back. The fight was to ensure that a private deal agreed earlier between ANC and NP negotiators – essentially that this all-powerful court be appointed by the cabinet – was replaced with something more constitutionally respectable. It was one of the few fights that had pitted our small party against the combined might of the 'big two' and, due to a public outcry and severe second thoughts on the issue by the outgoing NP government, on this matter, at least, we were winning.

Hence my appearance on TV, to report progress. As I entered the studio, the impeccably suited figure of Nelson Mandela, concluding his own interview, rose from his chair – somewhat stiffly – and fixed his beaming smile on me like a laser. 'Are you chaps making progress on the issue?' the great man enquired. I said I thought that we were. 'Well, I do hope so,' he responded. 'We must try to finish this thing tonight.'

Indeed, progress was made as the night wore on, and, in the early hours of the following morning, South Africa was handed a new interim constitution, and a looming date, five months hence, to elect its first democratic parliament.

While the wrangling continued almost until the last minute on a menu of items, other delegates who were not directly involved, the media, advisers and the umpteen hangers-on, had little to do but eat and drink, engage in speculative gossip or wander about to check on the progress being made by some of the key groups meeting in a variety of venues in the hangar-like building.

The helter-skelter nature of the process leading to that dramatic finale brought to mind the saying, 'if you like laws and sausages, you should never watch either one being made'. Some ascribe this remark to the late nineteenth-century 'Iron Chancellor' of Germany, Prince Otto von Bismarck, though others suggest this is a misattribution. Whoever said it could well have described the fraught, often rushed, and occasionally hair-raising negotiations that created South Africa's first democratic constitution, as much as the background of bloody, cacophonous events that marked the country's journey from the ending of apartheid to the first all-race election on 27 April 1994.

Despite the appearance of Mandela and De Klerk on the final night, neither of the leaders of the two principal parties – tribunes of the

coming power and the exiting one – was involved in the detailed discussions or the arm-wrestling over disputed issues when the talks were
in session. But they were the pivots around which the entire, often
ramshackle, process turned.

From my far lesser postion as a Democratic Party delegate, I was both
an engaged eyewitness and a sometimes direct participant in this roller-
coaster affair. I often had to remind myself, when tedium and frustration
induced irritation or boredom, that I was ringside at a very rare event: the
designing of a new constitution necessary for the reinvention of a country.
The title of US Secretary of State Dean Acheson's memoir, *Present at the
Creation*, seemed appropriate shorthand for this history-in-the-making.

From the vantage point of today, nearly two and a half decades later,
the crisp issue is the clues that Mandela and the ANC leadership offered
at the time on their approach to democracy, and quite how inclusive
and encompassing they intended it to be. Despite having enjoyed the
full-frontal warmth of the great man at our Houghton dinner party in
August 1992, I thought, even back then, that there was a fundamental
difference between our respective parties' approach to the issue. I did not
doubt Mandela's democratic impulses, but felt that many, perhaps most,
in his sprawling organisation simply viewed the coming constitution and
its processes as instruments to obtain political power, after which the
essence of democratic checks and balances – the restraints that effective
constitutional designs place on majoritarian decision-making – would
be either ignored or bypassed.

The constitutional negotiations did not of course occur in a vacuum.
All the parties in the negotiations, and their representatives, brought
their own histories, needs and expectations – baggage, as it were, that

many sought to reclaim in the very process unfolding and the documents then being inked. One colleague, whose identity I've now forgotten, buttonholed me after an intervention I was making during a plenary session and cautioned, 'Your point is well made, but we are not on Lake Geneva, you know; there is a looming revolution outside these doors and there isn't that much time to stop it.'

That appropriate warning jarred somewhat with what I thought to be the liberal approach to constitutionalism that had been embedded in my consciousness by my constitutional law lecturer at the University of Witwatersrand a decade or so before the Kempton Park negotiations. Professor Johan van der Vyver had trenchantly told our class, 'You should design a constitution with this in mind: will it restrain your worst enemy if he gets into power?'

Of equal relevance to the process of constitution-making were two other observations that seemed directly apposite – to me and others of the liberal school of thought – to this intermission time between South Africa's exclusion of the majority black population from political participation (the formal situation when negotiations commenced) and the overwhelming probability that their party of likely choice, Mandela's ANC, would win outright power at the first democratic election.

The first was the less-noted aphorism of the famous Lord Acton: 'The authority of the people must be restrained to safeguard freedom and the protection of minorities. The will of the people cannot make just that which is unjust.'

The second compelling observation – which was true of the racial fractures that had so wounded South Africa's past and likely would accompany it into the future, and which lay at the heart of the constitution-writing process – was made by the Belgian sociologist Pierre van den Berghe. What he wrote back in 1979 about Africa seemed crucially on-point to South Africa in the 1990s and the years beyond:

> If your constituency has the good fortune to contain a demographic majority, racism can be easily disguised as democracy. The ideological sleight of hand, is of course, that an ascriptive, racially-defined majority is a far cry from a majority made up of shifting coalitions of individuals … '[Majority] rule' in Africa can thus easily become a veneer for racial domination.[1]

These warnings had informed much of the constitutional thinking, such as 'consociational democracy', of my own political party during the 1980s when Dr Van Zyl Slabbert had been at its helm. However, they no longer enjoyed much currency by the time the negotiations commenced. Slabbert himself was an absent figure, having left parliamentary politics, and apparently no longer advanced this view.

The Democratic Party leadership, which in any event had little weight in the final decision-making at Kempton Park (we were just one of nineteen parties to the process and very much in the second tier of it), had largely become seized with the desire to midwife a successful outcome to the process itself. Despite my strenuous desire, shared by other 'young Turks' in the DP, for the party to be more robust on certain issues, the hierarchy seemed far happier, often, playing the role of facilitator and go-between.

The row about the judicial appointments was the exception to this approach. This meant that, on some quite crucial issues, or restraints on untrammelled majoritarianism, such as significant original powers for the provinces and the very drawing of the provincial boundaries them-selves, it often 'went along to get along'. The ANC was deeply suspicious of what it saw as attempts to restrain it once it was in power.

This left essentially the National Party, the exiting government, as latter-day converts and champions of the sort of constitutional checks and balances (such as super-majorities in both legislative and executive decision-making, strong minority vetoes and the decentralisation of power) it had once decried. For example, a decade or so before, when many similar measures had been proposed by the Natal Indaba of Mangosuthu Buthelezi, the NP government had dismissed them out of hand. Not for the first time, the NP's late acceptance ('a deathbed conversion' one wag named it) of such constitutional engineering provided proof of the phrase 'the fallacy of genesis'.

It was impossible to interrogate such ideas on their own merits; they became hostage to the view that other parties held about those advanc-ing them, and their motives in doing so. Indeed, Mandela, in response to a welter of NP proposals around the constitution, which De Klerk's gov-ernment termed *Deelnemende Demokrasie in 'n Regstaat* (Participatory Democracy in a Constitutional State), dismissed this scheme archly, per-haps accurately, as a 'loser takes all' system.[2]

In fact, the first draft of these NP proposals went far beyond anything conceived by liberal theorists: its model proposed a rotating presidency, shared between the leaders of the three-to-five largest parties, an all-party cabinet and a super-sized senate with disproportionate representation for minorities. Over time, the NP would drop most of these demands as the negotiations stalled.

Many years after the dust had settled on these talks, I attended a private dinner where NP chief negotiator Roelf Meyer explained that in his view these proposals were demands for continued white control or, at worst, 'co-governance'. He postulated that, only when the NP began to realise (persuaded by himself and some other senior officials) that it would have to relinquish these claims and settle for a bill of rights based on individual rights, could the process get back on track.

But the ambition of the initial NP demands was not the only stumbling block. The resumed enmity between the NP and ANC was primary: this had been briefly suspended in the afterglow of De Klerk's 2 February 1990 speech and the first meeting between the parties at Groote Schuur in Cape Town, but had long been supplanted with mistrust. This stemmed from multiple causes. Chief among them was the violence racking the townships and suburban trains (which, in the ANC view, the state was either complicit in or indifferent to).

From the government side there was the ANC's ambivalence around the armed struggle. After much wrangling over the movement's refusal to lay down arms, the Pretoria Minute signed between De Klerk and Mandela in August 1990 signalled the cessation of the armed struggle by the liberation movement's military wing, Umkhonto we Sizwe. But the continued existence and discovery of arms caches and guerrillas and secret operations (Operation Vula being the best known) suggested that this commitment had been honoured in the breach.

The rapid alienation of Buthelezi from both the government and the ANC and, over time, from the process itself, was another obstacle. In fact, Buthelezi, until then, had been a deft operator between the two systems vying for ascendancy: under the apartheid order of homelands, his position as chief minister of KwaZulu in Natal allowed him a legal political base and he held sway in much of the province. His opposition to the same system simultaneously marked him out as very different from most other homeland satraps and had ensured him a significant local following and many international admirers, not least of them the Prime Minister of Great Britain, Margaret Thatcher.

But his Inkatha movement was locked in a violent battle with Mandela's ANC, both in Natal and, increasingly, across the Reef in Johannesburg's townships. He had also been discredited in the run-up to the Convention for a Democratic South Africa (Codesa) by revelations that Inkatha had received secret government funding, and its paramilitaries covert defence force assistance. For all this he was arguably the person best positioned to advance the cause of federalism. But he never attended Kempton Park in person (after his demand for a separate delegation for the King of the Zulus had been declined); after a while, he withdrew his party delegation, believing the original principles agreed to there, especially the word 'undivided' in its description of a democratic South Africa, precluded the federal option.

The extraordinarily complex relationship between Buthelezi and Mandela was a running feature of those times, and one that would continue in later years, as I was to witness for myself. But throughout the unfolding political drama Buthelezi was, at best, the 'third man'.

South Africans had an early glimpse of the fraught relationship between the 'big two' on the centre stage of politics the moment Codesa first opened for official business on 20 December 1991. But the first spat between Mandela and De Klerk would show the many sides, and faces, of Mandela himself – something with which I, and a host of others, would become familiar in the future.

CHAPTER FOUR

Ascendance

Codesa started with a misunderstanding that morphed into the first dressing-down the nation ever witnessed of a white president by a black man, and a former prisoner to boot. It was to establish the template for the uneasy relationship between Mandela and De Klerk, who, like feuding conjoined twins, were unhappily but ineluctably joined at the hip by a process that both needed to succeed.

But that evening Codesa's progress seemed anything except assured. Perhaps the ablest chronicler of those times, Patti Waldmeir, the *Financial Times* correspondent and author of the subsequent book on the transition, *Anatomy of a Miracle,* best describes what South Africa and the world witnessed:

> Never had South Africa heard a black man speak to a white man
> that way – with the disgust and loathing, the scorn and venom of

centuries. Mandela, the master of self-discipline, lost all restraint …
As de Klerk sat listening, Mandela put the white president in his place
and then pinned him on the spot, with insult after insult. De Klerk
was the 'head of an illegitimate, discredited, minority regime', a man
who could not even be trusted to live up to its low moral standards. He was guilty of duplicity, trickery, lying, a man with 'very little
idea of what democracy means'. The kindest thing that could be said
of him was that he was 'a product of apartheid', and even that was
no excuse. He was 'not fit to be a head of government' … The fiery
Mandela temper, held in check through twenty-seven years of prison
indignities, exploded with the full force of long suppression.[1]

And, the author added, 'if Mandela had his way, [De Klerk] would not
long remain in that post'.

The background to that famous and very public dressing-down is
now long forgotten. It all related to events following the Pretoria Minute
in August 1990, when, as mentioned, an agreement was struck for the
ANC to suspend its armed struggle. Up until the night before the opening of Codesa, ANC and government negotiators had been locked in
disagreement over why the ANC had not placed its arms caches under
joint control. In Mandela's view, to have done so before the movement
itself was part of government would have been 'suicide'. On the failure
to reach an accord on this deadlock, the government chief negotiator,
Justice Minister Kobie Coetsee, told the ANC that De Klerk would raise
the matter in public the next day. This message apparently never reached
Mandela. When De Klerk used his speaking turn the next evening –
which Mandela had agreed would be the last speech of the event – to do

so, Mandela's spontaneous reply was based on the assumption that he had been tricked into allowing De Klerk the last word.

But, within moments of his outburst, Mandela showed another side: '[He] went out of his way to make peace with his rival, crossing the floor to shake De Klerk's hand – and making sure the gesture was captured by the same TV cameras which had recorded his earlier tirade.'[2]

It was apparent from then on that the relationship between the two – by far the most important politicians in the land – was, if not in a state of irretrievable breakdown, foundering on mutual mistrust. For Mandela, De Klerk's conduct and the issue that sparked it 'was proof of a double agenda' to destroy the ANC – disarm it and then collude with Inkatha and the security forces to attack its supporters. He also believed the president had little idea, and no understanding, of the pain and heat Mandela and Slovo and other key leaders had taken within their movement to suspend the armed struggle, theoretical though it might have been (both the efficacy of the armed resistance and the process of disarmament) at that stage. Many in the movement, his heroic credentials notwithstanding, regarded Mandela as a 'sell-out' for preferring his personal diplomacy with De Klerk to the barricades of struggle.[3]

De Klerk had his own pressures from his constituency too, who were being fed the line from the right-wing Conservative Party (which boycotted the opening of the talks) and key members of the security establishment that the president was 'soft' and too yielding to the might of the ANC.

But, whatever the misperceptions the one had of the other, Mandela's public lashing of De Klerk had perceptibly altered the terms of trade between the two men and the movements they led.

It is fair to say that, in the nearly two years between Mandela's release and the opening of Codesa, the momentum had been with President De Klerk. He was the head of an intact and powerful government and had the formal levers of power in his clutches and an ever-widening circle of international admirers in the Western leadership – from Germany's Helmut Kohl to America's George HW Bush and Britain's Margaret Thatcher and her successor, John Major – more or less on his side.

Mandela was tasked at the age of seventy-two with taking control of the leadership of his ramshackle organisation, which, after the first flush of its legalisation, was mired in organisational challenges, tactical differences and inchoate policy positions. He had barely been allowed the chance to regain a semblance of personal normality after decades of incarceration. Not least among his problems was having to contend with an unravelling marriage to Winnie, herself recently convicted of and facing imprisonment on four counts of kidnapping. Even Job in the Old Testament would have found Mandela's hardships difficult to accept – but, in addition, as the ANC's greatest political asset, Mandela had to patch quarrels, and worse, in his party and family, and was also required to criss-cross the globe, to advance his movement's cause and fill its coffers.

Not simply because Mandela stood his ground, and more, at Codesa, but also because, once the negotiations had started, the political relationship began to shift (from the terrain and edifices of parliamentary white politics to the new ground zero of negotiations), that December evening dressing-down in Kempton Park was the first of several turning points that South Africa would witness in the next two and a half years until its first democratic elections. And all of them, one or two false dawns apart, would indicate a profound tilt in the balance of power – and the power was shifting decisively in the direction of the ANC.

I have previously written at some length about the details and drama of the constitutional negotiations process, and many, perhaps more objective, chronicles of that period were published soon afterwards and still make compelling reading, especially from the vantage point of today.[4] However, the standout feature of that time remains for me one of unresolved wonderment: how was it that the initiative shifted so decisively to an obviously better-prepared and -led insurgency, the ANC, away from the government of the day? The facile, in part true, answer would be the forces and sweep of history that so favoured and fuelled the anti-government and thus anti-apartheid legions led by Mandela. But this does not fully explain why the ANC was, at most times in the process, better prepared and more tactically astute and strategically adept than the leaden-footed government negotiators appeared to be.

Some years later, when I was discussing this conundrum with the late business statesman Harry Oppenheimer, a lifelong student both of politics and of politicians, he offered an interesting observation, no doubt gleaned from his own time in parliament in the 1950s when apartheid was at its zenith: 'I think the National Party had an assumption steeped in years in power and in the racist policies they pursued and the views they held; they could not possibly be out-negotiated by blacks.' And then he added with a mischievous laugh, 'But they were, weren't they?'

Of course it was not just a racial prism that perhaps distorted the view of the outgoing government. The forces ranged against them at Codesa and afterwards had a specific agenda and a deep bench of negotiators on which to draw. The same ANC conference, which in July

1991 elected Mandela as its president, had also chosen, apparently against Mandela's wishes (he preferred to retain the somewhat somnambulant incumbent Alfred Nzo in the post),[5] mineworkers' union boss, the astute Cyril Ramaphosa, as secretary general. Soon enough he was appointed its lead negotiator, and was assisted in this task by a range of high-level functionaries and thinkers, including Mac Maharaj, Valli Moosa, Pravin Gordhan and the redoubtable Joe Slovo. Thabo Mbeki was less directly involved but played a key behind-the-scenes role too. Their backgrounds – in the unions, local activism, exile and prison – and collective intellects were as varied as they were impressive.

The ANC had also by then conquered most of civil society in the country, the business sector perhaps withstanding (and they soon enough detected which way the winds of power were shifting and made their accommodations accordingly). Thus, when Codesa went about appointing technical committees, secretariats and the like, the ANC and forces aligned with it could call on a rich, often glittering, pool of talent from the universities, the legal profession and non-governmental organisations to assist it and advance its agenda.

It was not simply a question of people and organisations electing to be on 'the right side of history'. The NP had been steeped in government for nearly five decades, and had acquired expertise in, and all the habits of, administration, and not too many perspectives outside those of a labyrinthine bureaucracy. It was no doubt difficult for it to shed its executive mindedness for an entirely different world view, one that would be needed to protect its voters against the might of a future government, the very antithesis of its own approach imbued in a lifetime of power.

While De Klerk's bold-sweep announcements had caught his opponents on the hop at the time they were made in early 1990, it had also flat-footed his own side. Very soon after the negotiations proper commenced, it would become clear that the government side had few bottom lines that, subject to pressure – often extreme, it should be noted – would not be yielded. It became apparent that De Klerk was a master tactician, but not an astute strategist, to whom one could, perhaps, apply British journalist Jonathan Freedland's description of Israeli strongman leader Ariel Sharon: 'He could see the next hill ... but he could not ... grasp the entire mountain range.'[6]

And the pathfinders his government chose to navigate the new political terrain were not up to the task, for a medley of reasons: their first senior negotiator, Gerrit Viljoen, a classicist and a senior minister who commanded considerable respect on all sides, had some form of nervous collapse and quit Codesa and politics soon after its commencement; his interim replacement was a deputy minister, Dr Tertius Delport, who lacked both the authority and, especially in establishing cordial relations with his adversaries, the ease of manner of his predecessor.

Ultimately, De Klerk entrusted this task to the well-mannered and soft-spoken Roelf Meyer, who had commenced his political life steeped in the conservative mind-set of his own background and party. But, like his political bosses, he had tracked to the middle, reformist, ground where De Klerk had, in recent times, pitched his political tent. However, time would reveal him to be unequal to the fairly brutal negotiating tactics of his ANC opponents. Perhaps, again, Meyer had no fixed ideology and his tractability as the process unfolded was mirrored some years later. He fell out with De Klerk in 1996, quit the

NP and, after his brief attempt to start a new political movement (the United Democratic Movement, with Bantu Holomisa) failed, threw in his lot with the ANC.

When I was visiting Washington DC during the negotiations process, De Klerk's ambassador there, a one-time colleague in the parliamentary opposition, Harry Schwarz, told me that he had telephoned De Klerk and suggested, 'Why don't you simply go to the Johannesburg Bar[7] and hire four or five of the best senior counsel there? They are likely to get a better result for you.' De Klerk did not heed his ambassador's advice; over time, his harried senior ministers at the negotiations would be rushed from one session to another, very often late at night, and during the day had government ministries to run. I found it extraordinary, for example, towards the finalisation of the interim constitution, that one man, the enigmatic Kobie Coetsee, held both the key portfolios of Justice and Defence, around which many of the unresolved and critical issues were located, and had to be the lead negotiator on them both, often forcing the adjournment of the one committee to hasten off to the other. In contrast, the ANC was far better organised and generally better prepared.

It was not, however, one-way traffic in Mandela and the ANC's direction. After the opening spat at Codesa, the negotiators agreed to a set of principles. One of them gave the liberation movement a key concession: Codesa would write the interim constitution but an elected constitutional assembly, after the first democratic poll, would draft the final document. But De Klerk reckoned that he could spin out the interim phase until he had achieved in the interim process binding commitments for blocking mechanisms that would prevent the final constitution being simply a green light for 'simple majority rule'. By achieving 'permanent power-sharing' in the first document, his party could then fetter un-restrained majoritarianism into the foreseeable future. The ANC, of course, had a very different outcome in mind, and it was left to five working groups to design the necessary compromises between these dia-metrically opposed approaches.

I was appointed an 'adviser' to the DP delegation to the most sig-nificant of these groups, Working Group Two, whose purpose was to thrash out, in lengthy sessions between January the following year and a self-imposed mid-May 1992 deadline, the essence of how South Africa was to be governed in the future – specifically, what percentages would be required to enact legislation, especially the final constitution itself, and how would the NP desire for power-sharing be institutionalised?

As much time was spent, due to delays and 'the need to caucus', outside the formal sessions, enjoying the lavish and free (except for the unsuspecting taxpayers who footed the bill) catering facilities of the World Trade Centre. This allowed the different sides to meet and chat in more relaxed, less adversarial surrounds. It was in such circumstances that my own initial antipathy to Slovo, for example, melted as I found his sharp and cynical humour made us, across the divide of age and ideology, actually quite kindred spirits. During one such chat, I complimented him on some or other move that had helped unjam the process, to which he rejoined, 'Well, that's what comes from all those nights around the poker table. It's the best place to learn strategy!' Ramaphosa exuded a charm of his own, but struck me, despite the ready smile and easy laugh, as pretty calculating and probing, doubtless essential attributes for a successful negotiator.

For all the superficial bonhomie and banter, there was no disguising the looming collision between the deadline and the deadlock on the essential issues. At that stage, it appeared the NP government had the wind behind its back. In March, De Klerk had won an overwhelming referendum victory of nearly 70 per cent of the white electorate in favour of proceeding with the constitutional process. This again proved him the master tactician: he had used the humiliation of an earlier by-election loss to the ultra-right-wing Conservative Party in his own university town of Potchefstroom (in the western Transvaal) as a pivot to call the bluff of the forces of conservatism.

CHAPTER FIVE

Democratic Imperative

DE KLERK'S REFERENDUM win was an emphatic repudiation, by whites at least, of the scorched-earth prospectus of the far right. But it probably deceived him, and his negotiators, into drawing the wrong strategic conclusion: that time was on their side. They could now outmanoeuvre the ANC and, perhaps, even cobble together some or other coalition of forces to beat them – if not at an all-race election, then in the negotiating chamber.

At that stage, the parties at Codesa (many representing the grab bag of homeland governments) were fairly evenly split between the ANC and NP, at least on certain issues. It was quite striking to observe the NP negotiators dig in their heels on the arithmetical question: what percentage would be required for the future constitutional assembly to approve the new constitution? By then, it had been agreed that the unelected Codesa would write the interim one and would also frame the principles to which the final document would have to conform. It had also been agreed that more than 50 per cent of the new assembly would have to approve it.

But the devil in the detail here was the threshold that the final constitution and the all-important Bill of Rights would have to clear: was it to be two thirds, or 70 per cent, or some combination depending on the sections involved? The higher the threshold, of course, the better off the future minority parties would be and the more disadvantaged the new ruling party. The NP proposed an elaborate mechanism for two tiers of voting: two thirds for most of the constitution, but a three-quarters majority on the matters closest to its political heart: the Bill of Rights, federalism and minority rights.

The ANC balked at this. While the formal session of Codesa was waiting to start on 15 May 1992, our working group was presented with Ramaphosa's counteroffer, in its own way as unacceptable to his adversaries as the NP bid: 70 per cent for all clauses of the constitution and three quarters for the Bill of Rights. But then he added the fatal rider: if the elected assembly could not, in six months, agree to a constitution, a referendum of all voters would be held where a simple 50 per cent majority would approve it. The NP rejected this, a deadlock ensued, and the plenary was postponed to the next day. Patti Waldmeir describes what happened next, out of sight of the delegates:

> Mandela and de Klerk met that night over coffee. They knew Codesa was a disaster, but they did not dare admit it publicly, fearing the consequences if the peace process was seen to have stalled. They agreed to declare victory, and withdraw. The next day in his closing address,

> Mandela praised the 'remarkable job' done by Codesa and portrayed the delegates as members of a happy multiracial family, while de Klerk congratulated the gathering for having turned a crisis into a triumph. Codesa II [as the conference became known] ended with a vain attempt to trick the populace into thinking all was well.[1]

In fact Codesa would never reconvene, at least not under that name. And in the eighteen months following that day and the finalisation of the interim constitution in November 1993, at the same venue under the banner of the Multi-Party Negotiation Process, South Africa would be buffeted by extremes of political weather. This would include racking violence, mass action, summits and more violence, the political assassination of senior ANC and SA Communist Party leader Chris Hani, and an attempted putsch in the homeland of Bophuthatswana.

The hugely consequential eight months in 1993 between the resumption of the constitutional talks in April and its finalisation in November were not all about nonstop negotiations in the public eye. There were plenary or public sessions, but most of the work was done in small meeting rooms among key participants wrestling with the standout issues. Fate decreed that my committee, charged with thrashing out a bill of rights, was not meeting on the day when probably the most dramatic of all moments in a long-run power play occurred at Kempton Park. In late June[2] the extreme right-wing forces of the Afrikaner Weerstandsbeweging (AWB), led by the buffoonish but sinister Eugene Terre'Blanche, briefly took over the talks venue, after invading it with an armoured car and men on horseback. These latter-day burghers succeeded in smashing part of the glazed facade of the building, and, for a while, took charge as delegates scurried outside to safety. But, as with other right-wing ruses of the time, the sound and fury of it did little to retard the momentum of the process.

Those months would, in fact, affirm the essential truth of the shifting power balance. The root misconception that bedevilled the NP strategy was its belief that a slow transition to power-sharing would trump the ANC's plan for a speedy road to majority rule. In fact, every surge of violence made a settlement more urgent, and, while the NP had the formal levers of power at its disposal, the ANC had effective leadership of the masses, and De Klerk and the ever-watchful international community would not countenance unrestrained force against them. Every concession De Klerk gave to the ANC simply alienated him further from the one man and party he could perhaps have aspired to coalesce with, Buthelezi and Inkatha.

Buthelezi had by then thrown in his lot with the rejectionist right-wingers, another forlorn strategy that yielded him few results except cementing his image of futile defiance of a process from which he had largely excluded himself.

Nothing illustrated this better than the final fate of the vexed question of percentages: ultimately, the NP caved in and accepted a flat two thirds on all sections of the constitution. Even the power-sharing compromise it wrought – for a multiparty cabinet of national unity and one of two deputy state presidencies for the leader of the largest minority party – was fatally undermined by its further concession: an agreement to fix power-sharing only for the life of the interim constitution (two years) and that decision-making in the cabinet would be, effectively, on a majoritarian basis.

Waldmeir's later chronicle of what happened after the first deadlock back at Codesa II confirmed my own eyewitness account of the momentous, and often searing, times and events that followed:

> De Klerk ought to have known that the deal would inevitably deteriorate over time, as the balance of power shifted inexorably toward the ANC. But he did not then subscribe to the 'take what you can get' school of negotiation. He was on a roll, he had power, and he was happy to do no more than talk about sharing it. Where he had gambled and won on the referendum, he gambled and lost at Codesa. De Klerk's luck deserted him there; it would never reappear.[3]

That vividly describes the miscalculation of one of the political conjoined twins that the negotiations process had uneasily joined together. What of the role of the other half – Nelson Mandela? Key ANC negotiator Mac Maharaj explained Mandela's role as being unyielding on the key issue of majority rule, but accommodating on providing some reassurance to the white minority: "'His zig-zags were always leading to the same object … When I went to see him, he would ask, 'Where does that take us towards majority rule? How long will it take?'" Maharaj described Mandela as "'my compass, through all the talks'" and noted, archly, "'The Nats [Nationalists] had no compass; in the end they became preoccupied with their selfish interests.'"[4]

One day in the last week of the talks, as we were finalising the key Bill of Rights section of the constitution, Sheila Camerer, the elegant NP member of our small committee, made a telling offhand corridor remark to me and the sharp-eared *Sunday Times* reporter Edyth Bulbring. 'I'm here to give away the family silver,' she said, 'but I'm going to do so with a smile on my face.' Unfortunately for Sheila, but happily for posterity, those words were splashed on the front page of the next Sunday's edition.

Far earthier was the response of the more hardline NP minister Dr Tertius Delport, who had been dropped early on by De Klerk to make way for the more conciliatory Roelf Meyer. In an incident he confirmed to me many years later when we were in the same political party, Delport famously grabbed De Klerk's lapels at a cabinet briefing the morning after the negotiations had ended, and demanded: 'What have you done? You've given the country away!'

An objective reading of the final draft accords with these assessments. The NP obtained limited power-sharing at executive level for the duration of the first parliament and in the provinces, and job security or retirement packages for senior civil servants. The critical issue of amnesty for security force officers (and for ANC combatants) was agreed to in principle, and the Bill of Rights protected vital minority interests, especially property ownership. Certainly, it was not the outright 'seizure of power' about which uncompromising insurrectionists in Mandela's movement fantasised. But, on the key issue of majority rule, unfettered by permanent minority blocking mechanisms, an unyielding Mandela had won.

In many ways, however, De Klerk's position was the most difficult: he was, in essence, surrendering power, and the momentum was with his opponents. He did so contrary to prediction and, particularly, the weight and expectation of his own people and party's history. In my view, he fully deserved to share the 1993 Nobel Prize he was jointly awarded with Mandela towards the end of that momentous year.

Nothing demonstrated the passage of power more fundamentally than the hinge event on which the country nearly tipped into insurrection: the assassination by two white right-wing extremists, one an immigrant from Communist Poland, of Chris Hani on Easter Saturday, 10 April 1993, amidst another protracted wrangle at the negotiating table. De Klerk, who was on holiday, was an absent figure, but certainly not an insensitive one. As he later recalled, '"This was Mandela's moment not mine"'.[5]

There were two immediate consequences in the aftermath of this terrible event. Mandela, in a dramatic speech on national television, achieved a preternatural poise that sucked some of the hatred out of the atmosphere. He said: "A white man, full of prejudice and hate, came to our country and committed a deed so foul that our whole nation teeters on the brink of disaster. A white woman, of Afrikaner origin, risked her life so that we may know, and bring to justice, this assassin."[6]

But in the gathering uncertainty and spreading violence that followed, Mandela's negotiators obtained the most significant concession when the talks resumed: the date of the election, 27 April 1994.

In the month before that historic date, the turning of the tide was vividly expressed in a bloody event in one of the most remote outposts of the country, hundreds of kilometres away from the centres of political power and the heat of township violence. It was not merely that the would-be invasion of the homeland of Bophuthatswana in March 1994 by AWB heavies, led by Eugene Terre'blanche, was aborted. Nor that Lucas Mangope, the homeland leader whose cry for assistance they were answering, was frustrated in his forlorn attempt not to hold elections in his territory. Rather, it was the execution-style murder of three

AWB members by the homeland police force, caught close-up by television cameras, that sent out an electrifying signal. The scenes broadcast that night on SABC TV were unmistakable in their meaning; the price of resistance to the democratic juggernaut was every bit as high as the dreams of separatist outcomes were delusional. South Africa would shortly have a new government.

When the nation cast its ballots, around twenty million of them, the following month, they would, in overwhelming numbers, propel Mandela to the presidency.

CHAPTER SIX

Breakfast with the President

I SAT SPELLBOUND along with the 200 other guests in the stately banqueting hall of the Mount Nelson Hotel in Cape Town as the internationally acclaimed soprano Barbara Hendricks delivered an electrifying rendition of the spiritual 'He's got the whole world in his hands', beaming a meaningful look at the man at the centre of it all.

It was June 1994 and Nelson Mandela, newly elected as president, was hosting his first state banquet for his first official foreign guest, French President François Mitterrand, a glittering moment in which the sentiment of that song seemed a pitch-perfect summary of the first few months of the new era. The refrain was as much a statement about Mandela as it was a reflection of how the world viewed him and the country that he now led.

But in a star-crossed life crowded with finest hours and consequential moments, and the years in the pit of struggle and despair, it was probably the four weeks, between the election on 27 April 1994 and his first address to the new parliament on 24 May, that must have been the most significant for Mandela.

In that momentous month, he was inaugurated as president at the Union Buildings in Pretoria before the leaders of an admiring world and citizens of a country that appeared to have crossed centuries of division and conflict into a brave new world that its leader powerfully symbolised. Nothing at his inauguration better reflected this, perhaps, than the crisp salutes he received on the podium from the armed service chiefs, and the fly-past by the SA Air Force; both the generals and the aircraft had until quite recently been deployed to destroy the organisation Mandela led.

A warm glow suffused the commencement of his presidency as Mandela went about forming his Government of National Unity, consisting of ministers from parties that had attained more than 5 per cent of the national vote, or twenty seats in parliament. The ANC, which obtained over 62 per cent of the vote and seats, dominated the cabinet.

The new arrangements provided some significant consolation prizes for the runners-up as well. De Klerk and the NP were dismayed with their 20 per cent of the overall total, but doubtless were consoled that this entitled them to one of two deputy presidencies (Thabo Mbeki being the other) and half a dozen national ministries. The party also won the province of the Western Cape with an outright majority.

Ministerial fortune shone, too, on the recalcitrant Buthelezi, whose last-minute decision to contest the election, announced just a week before polling day, secured his Inkatha Freedom Party (IFP) control of the province of KwaZulu-Natal and national ministries for him and two colleagues.

Conspicuously absent from these power-sharing arrangements and the perquisites that went with them was the Democratic Party, the home and inheritor of South Africa's liberal tradition. We had been comprehensively smashed between the hammer of African nationalism and the anvil of minority fears about the new order. Many of our traditional supporters deserted us – some aligning themselves with the ANC, harbingers of a new democratic order as they conceived it, but most abandoning us for the NP, believing that De Klerk and his party would be the strongest protector of their interests. Around 350 000 out of twenty million voters stood fast with the DP. This secured us just seven seats in the new parliament and a scattering of provincial representatives in five legislatures of the nine newly delimited provinces.

This dire result forced the resignation of our gentlemanly, but somewhat detached, leader Zach de Beer. On 22 May 1994, just two days before Mandela's first address to parliament, a shell-shocked and diminished party council elected me – one of the few MPs to make it back into parliament – as the acting leader (the party congress later in the year unanimously confirmed me in the position).

I surveyed our shipwreck with a combination of determination and dread. On one hand, I was seized with a zeal to stamp our distinctive mark on the new politics, believing the party had spent far too much of its political capital on facilitating a constitutional convergence and far too little on providing a clear blue-water alternative to fire up its supporters. I also knew that I had won the contest for the leadership against Ken Andrew because my pugnacious stance across the election campaign inspired some hope that I could lead a revival. On the other hand, I knew that, with just 1.7 per cent of the seats in parliament, we would battle for relevance – and even to be heard in the chamber, let alone outside it.

The feel-good, let's-all-pull-together emotion now sweeping the country would find my more adversarial approach to politics jarring. Yet the very go-along-to-get-along approach that the party had hitherto adopted had, in my view at least, cost us a lot of votes and had shrunk our political purpose. Even our reduction in numbers had not, at this early stage, resulted in a unity of purpose, and many in the party councils were uncertain about how the party should position itself – or whether it would survive at all.

The media was universally scornful of our future prospects and there was little in the way of donor enthusiasm for our cause. I decided – outwardly at least – to adopt the mien expressed in the famous battlefield despatch of French Marshal Foch during the First Battle of the Marne in September 1914: 'My centre is giving way, my right is in retreat: situation excellent. I shall attack.' But I had some real doubts about whether I, and the cause I was now entrusted to lead, could succeed.

Such uncertainties stood to one side as I entered the chamber of parliament on 24 May, the day of Mandela's first address. Whatever I felt as a politician about our own diminished place in it, as a citizen it seemed wondrous that here, in the very place of their historic exclusion, hundreds of newly minted black MPs now milled about. They ranged from the famous of prison, exile and the trade union movement, to the obscure. But they, like us holdovers from the last parliament, were seized with an equal sense of historic awe and anticipation.

Mandela, in truth usually a rather dull speaker, roused himself and his oratory to meet the expectations of the House and the many listening to him beyond its confines that day. In what he described as a 'glorious vision', he quoted the words of a poem by the late dissident Afrikaans poet Ingrid Jonker:

The child is not dead
The child lifts his fists against his mother
Who shouts Africa! …
The child is not dead
Not at Langa nor at Nyanga
Nor at Orlando nor at Sharpeville …

Mandela's choice of poet and her recitation of sites of struggle by Africans was instructive. But so was his forward-looking message that the government that he now led needed, both because of and despite its history, to be 'inspired by the single vision of creating a people-centred society'. He struck a deep chord with me, and underscored the inclusivity he now championed, when he said the government would use as its yardstick the 'freedom of the individual' encased in guarantees of political and human rights for 'all our citizens'.[1]

Shortly after he had finished I sent a note to him across the House, warmly congratulating him on his election and expressing the hope that the DP could be of service in the new South Africa. I added, as an after-thought, that perhaps we could meet at some stage 'to develop a creative dialogue on the road ahead'.

The letter was sincere, though strictly speaking a courtesy, and I expected no response. That very evening, however, the telephone rang while I was pottering about my mother's Camps Bay holiday flat, a Cape

Town base, in the company of Douglas Gibson, our chief whip, who was lodging with me until his own apartment was ready. It was about 10pm. I was stunned – at this relatively late hour, I hardly expected it to be the new president, better known for his early turn-ins. But there he was, chuckling on the other end of the phone, this hero of the world calling the leader of a minor opposition party for a chat. He talked at some length about his appreciation for my sentiments, asked warmly after certain DP figures, and then invited me to join him for breakfast at his Cape Town residence in two days' time.

I presented myself at the white-gabled Cape Dutch mansion that sits atop the rather grand and rolling Groote Schuur estate in Rondebosch, the residential precinct in Cape Town for the president and numerous cabinet ministers. I had never entered its hallowed portals before and, on being seated in a vast and impersonal lounge while waiting to be summoned to break bread with the president, I was at once struck by the four bulky chandeliers that dominated the room, and the rather less elegant vestige of a party the night before of dirty ashtrays and glasses. This stood in stark contrast to the beautiful manicured lawns and gardens immediately outside the reception room.

After a brief wait I was escorted upstairs to a small dining room, where an impeccably groomed Mandela welcomed me with his famous smile. Accompanied only by his secretary, Mary Mxadana, and an over-anxious Air Force chef, we sat down to spanspek, oats and scrambled egg for me, and (I couldn't but note it as a reflection of our respective waistlines) just toast and jam for the president. I was quite fascinated to watch Mandela make a sandwich of his buttered toast and cut it carefully, precisely in the middle, a far more graceful exercise than anything I attempted with the breakfast now displayed in front of me.

Mandela was exceptionally welcoming, full of personal praise for my 'leadership ability', and pronounced himself determined to enjoy a close relationship with the DP. I found it interesting that he singled out Harry Schwarz as 'a champion of the poor' – essentially correct in my estimation, but contrary to the old Prog (Progressive Party) caricature of the then-ambassador to Washington and former member of parliament for Yeoville, as a 'right-wing hawk'. I, too, spoke warmly of Schwarz, who had played an oscillating role in my own political rise. He was also known in his heyday for the intensity of his often-difficult personality. I recounted to Mandela a jibe made about Schwarz by the former president PW Botha, who once said of him, 'The problem with the honourable member for Yeoville is that he wants to be the bride at every wedding and the corpse at every funeral.' Mandela roared with laughter.

I felt bad about the fact that Zach de Beer had fallen on his sword, and would indeed spend most of my subsequent years in leadership ensuring that former leaders of the party were recognised and honoured where possible. So I thought that morning to put in a plug for my vanquished predecessor. I suggested to Mandela that Zach would make 'a fine diplomat', an entreaty subsequently taken up by the president, who later appointed De Beer ambassador to the Netherlands.

What I found most revealing and refreshing was Mandela's openness and candour. When I spelt out how I saw our role as a 'loyal opposition', he immediately agreed on the need for such a parliamentary watchdog, but assured me that on all major issues there tended to be huge areas of disagreement within the ANC itself. Pivots of division vested in a triad of former Robben Island prisoners, the formerly exiled leadership, and the internal activists. These elements comprised the ANC's own (self-sealed) 'opposition'.

For some reason, Mandela introduced the subject and complex personality of Inkatha president Mangosuthu Buthelezi, who seemed in our later talks a semi-permanent presence in the mind of Madiba. He launched into an essentially psychological deconstruction of his opponent from KwaZulu-Natal, telling me that to understand Buthelezi you had to appreciate his past, especially his childhood. He described at some length to me that Buthelezi was 'only the son of a chief'.[2] According to the history presented by Mandela that morning, there was some fear on the part of Buthelezi's mother that her young son was at risk from 'local sorcerers and witchdoctors', and so he was sent to the royal kraal of her brother, the King of the Zulus, Solomon kaDinizulu. In the palace, according to Mandela, Buthelezi was 'ignored and lonely'. This, the president advised, had left Buthelezi with a 'lifelong insecurity', which played itself out in his sharp alterations of both mood and behaviour.

I was tempted to tell Mandela that, if he looked into my own background, with my mother's multiple divorces, he might also find the origins of my personal anxieties and insecurities – but thought better of it! We concluded our discussion more than an hour and a quarter later. What shone through for me was how well grounded he was; as the French say: 'he wore his own skin'. I couldn't help thinking that he must have had impressive and deeply nurturing parents.

Of course, by embracing me in his circle of confidence, he presumably figured on inoculating himself against any prospect of personal attack. Not that the world, or South Africa, would have taken much notice had I been stupid enough to take him on. However, I decided that I would not allow myself to become a sort of pet poodle placed on the opposition benches. Part of the DP's past mistakes had flowed from a desperate desire to be affirmed by the liberation camp.

An interesting by-product of that first presidential meeting with Mandela and the essential result of it – a posting abroad for my predecessor – led me directly to meet shortly thereafter with Mandela's right hand in government, Deputy President Thabo Mbeki. The ostensible purpose of that early encounter with Mbeki was to try to find out how arrangements for Zach's posting were progressing. Mbeki, as deputy president, was in reality the de facto head of government. (My colleague Colin Eglin referred to Mandela as the 'Lord Mayor of Africa' and to Mbeki as the 'country's CEO' – an astute observation.)

In contrast to his later metamorphosis into a chilly, distant eminence, dismissive of critics and often sneeringly sarcastic in his political approach, the Mbeki of 1994 was a much nicer person, far more approachable and accommodating. He was quite frank about 'the extremely slow and frustrating nature of cabinet' and the 'sheer weight of bureaucracy which pulled and directed government, rather than the other way around'. It was apparently in this process that Zach's nomination was ensnared.

Perhaps it was his early, unhappy encounter with labyrinthian procedures that helped firm Mbeki's later instincts for control and centralisation.

He also admitted that one of his greatest frustrations was the absence of time to pursue essential policy development and implementation. In the event, he kept his door wide open to me for the next four or so years (shortly after our meeting, Zach received his ambassadorial posting), but, thereafter, it was never to reopen until I stood down as party leader in May 2007.

However, in those now-distant but defining early days of democracy, the mood music between government and opposition – or at least the fraction of it that I led – was generally more harmonious than the raucous and often angry discourse that characterised it after Mandela exited office.

But, even back in 1994, Mandela showed that his famous bonhomie had clear limits; he did not like being crossed. So when, early in the new parliament, I interrogated his government on a massacre that had occurred just weeks before the election outside the ANC headquarters in downtown Johannesburg, the breakfast banter was replaced by something much angrier. Shell House was the name of the building at the time, but it also became a metaphor for something much darker, on which I was determined to shine some light.

Massacre Blowback

SEATED ON A couch just inches away from a fuming Nelson Mandela, I shifted uncomfortably as he launched into a rare full-frontal attack that revealed an aspect of his political persona I had not experienced first-hand until then.

'Well, of course, you're a young man and you want to make an impression,' the normally emollient president fulminated, 'but your party is essentially a white organisation!'

I had been summoned to the presidential office in Tuynhuys, abutting parliament, early one morning in May 1995 for another purpose, but Mandela used the occasion to vent his anger at what he obviously regarded as the temerity of the stance I had adopted on a highly controversial affair involving the ANC.

It was discomforting for me, to say the least, and it was clear from his increasingly angry features that he meant it to be.

'When we were on "the Island",'[1] he went on with some feeling, 'we followed the debates in parliament quite intensely. Often, with the exception of issues such as the armed struggle and sanctions, we found that the Progressive Party[2] and the ANC were on the same page. Now I find you are a right-wing party with a vendetta against the ANC!'

The path that led to this extraordinary and – compared with my previous encounters with Mandela – unprecedented dressing-down began some thirteen months before in downtown Johannesburg on a day of violence – 28 March 1994 – just under a month before the historic election.

I experienced the event, later dubbed the 'Shell House Massacre', firsthand. That morning, amidst my election campaigning activities, I was driving my car down Jeppe Street to the offices of the law firm Edward Nathan & Friedland, where I managed to do some legal work in between my more time-consuming focus on politics.

Without any warning, my journey towards the glass-and-concrete tower block in which the law firm's offices were situated was interrupted when my car was suddenly surrounded by hundreds of Zulu demonstrators in red bandanas, the colour of the Inkatha Freedom Party (IFP), swinging clubs, pangas and knobkieries. The mood was angry. It was a terrifying sight.

When the mob began to rock my car, and bang on the roof, denting it, I became very frightened. Just as I was beginning to contemplate my short life ending on the wrong side of one of the assegais some of the demonstrators were now thrusting at my closed window, two traffic officers miraculously materialised, and guided me into a side street. Shaken and somewhat stunned, I sped away and managed to beat a retreat to our offices.

Shortly afterwards, the office block was fired upon, and the massive glass entrance windows were shattered by stones. It was far more reassuring to watch the melee from the twenty-third floor than to experience it close-up at street level. But other unfortunate motorists caught up in the demonstration and I were simply collateral victims of the mob's fury. The real target was the ANC and their nearby national headquarters at Shell House, later to be renamed after Chief Albert Luthuli.

The background to the chaos on the streets lay in the increasingly poisoned wells of co-operation between Mandela and Buthelezi and their rival organisations. On the day of the march, Buthelezi was still boycotting the looming elections. He was also holding out against the new constitution that he and his then-ally King Goodwill Zwelithini believed diminished the powers of the Zulu royal house and its chiefs, the *amakhosi*. The downtown demonstration was apparently a rally in support of the king. During the later amnesty hearings of the Truth and Reconciliation Commission (TRC), counsel for the ANC claimed that the causes of the king were simply a 'smokescreen' for the IFP to 'cause chaos in Johannesburg'.[3]

By that day in late March, Mandela's efforts to charm Buthelezi into submission had failed. International mediators who arrived in town just weeks after the demonstration, led by former US Secretary of State Dr Henry Kissinger, were to be equally unsuccessful. Ultimately Buthelezi did contest the election, but that morning in Johannesburg seemed a harbinger of the violence to come, and any prospect of a peaceful election seemed far more distant than the date, just a few weeks away, for which it was set.

My encounter with the demonstrators was just a foretaste of the mayhem that soon engulfed Johannesburg, as some 20 000 surged towards Shell House and surrounding ANC offices. Eight of the demonstrators were shot and killed by ANC guards firing at them from Shell House. The ANC later claimed they were trying to storm the building; other eyewitnesses disagreed and one journalist besieged inside Shell House described it as a 'bloody counter attack'.[4] At the end of that day of carnage, which witnessed other gunfights in adjacent areas, fifty-three people, most of them demonstrators, lay dead.[5]

In the days that followed, I carefully read the claims and counter-claims around the event. Given the overwhelming likelihood that the ANC would form the next government, I took special note of how the organisation – effectively already a government-in-waiting – responded to the events and their aftermath. It was not at all reassuring. As Martin Meredith noted in his biography, 'the event also tarnished Mandela's reputation'.[6] He summarised the involvement of the likely next president in less than flattering terms:

> He was not present when Zulu demonstrators arrived outside Shell House, but the following day, when police wanted to search the premises for weapons and for forensic evidence, he personally refused to allow them entry. Asked later at a press conference if, in a new government, his law and order minister would allow political opponents to set conditions for police probes into criminal activity, he replied, 'Let's face that when we are the government. I am entitled to negotiate with law and order officials.' The Johannesburg *Sunday Times* observed caustically, 'What a rare achievement for the ANC. It has

succeeded in putting itself above the law before taking power. In most banana republics it happens the other way around.'[7]

What alarmed me at the time was less the event – for, on the bloody palimpsest of South Africa's transition, it was sadly just one of dozens of violent episodes – than the seemingly cavalier manner in which the ANC appeared to be obstructing the proper police investigation of it. At the time I had absolutely no idea of Mandela's role in the saga – this would only be revealed more than a year later. But I was troubled by what the event suggested for the future of the rule of law in the country, a key foundation stone of the new constitution.

After the election, I was cooling my heels in the same Johannesburg law offices – now happily without the angry mob down below – prior to my departure a few days hence for the first sitting of the new parliament in Cape Town, when I received a notice from the legislature advising me of the deadline for submitting the first batch of parliamentary questions. The Shell House shootings and their sequel seemed just the ticket for testing the commitment of our new political masters to transparent justice, so I faxed a series of questions back to Cape Town about the obstacles hampering the investigation.

A day or so later, I received a startling fax from a police colonel whom I knew slightly. He advised that his office was preparing the 'official parliamentary response' to my questions, but that the real facts of the matter would not be in the answers. He then pretty much gave me chapter and verse on what amounted to a comprehensive stitch-up and the frustration of the police investigation. It suggested, in some impressive detail, that the shootings were essentially unprovoked and unjustified. More alarming was the detail he provided on elements in the police hierarchy (scenting the impending change in power) having connived with the ANC leadership, including Mandela, to cover up the incident and protect the guilty.

On the first question day in parliament, in June, I waited for the response from the hapless new Minister of Safety and Security, Sydney Mufamadi. I chiefly wanted to know whether the police had been given unrestricted access to Shell House to obtain evidence, particularly of a ballistic nature.

On this issue, Mufamadi claimed: 'The police were not denied access to the building, but had themselves sought to rely on the co-operation of the ANC in order to facilitate their investigation.'

This I knew to be false. So I leapt up and read from the internal police memorandum that had been leaked to me: '[Because] the police could not access Shell House … no investigation was done inside and no one inside was asked any questions.'[8]

I also informed parliament I understood that no fewer than five different attempts had been made to obtain the ANC's co-operation – and that each had been rebuffed. I then read into the record a letter to the ANC from the police, which stated in part: 'It is understood that you have since withdrawn the undertaking to allow the police access to Shell House… [We] call on you to honour your initial undertaking and arrange that the firearms used during the incident be handed over forthwith.'[9]

Without the arrogance and evasiveness that came to characterise this minister and many of his colleagues in later years, Mufamadi replied rather lamely, 'Until this morning I was trying to get further information relating to this question, and I was assured by both parties that the commitment to co-operate still stood.'[10]

This was clearly contradicted by the facts in my possession. Douglas Gibson, our chief whip, put down a motion calling for an ad hoc select committee to be appointed 'to investigate whether Mufamadi had deliberately misled parliament with his answers'.

After some foot-dragging, a debate on the motion was held six weeks later, and the committee was duly appointed and convened. Although (with its in-built ANC majority) it exonerated the minister, the exercise had interesting consequences.

The first concerned Madiba – President Mandela. My questions and the acres of press coverage they received clearly grated. Shortly after my joust with Mufamadi, I received a request from the president's office to meet with him 'and to bring my whole caucus'. This was not a particularly difficult feat, since, all found (with our three senators included), we numbered just ten souls.

There was as little amity at this initial meeting as there would be some months later at our one-on-one showdown. In front of my colleagues, he berated me, and then rather startled our small group by advising that he had, via telephone apparently, personally instructed the ANC guards to 'defend our headquarters', since the 'IFP was on its way to kill us all'.

None of the ANC guards were ever charged, and the lack of co-operation between the party and the police continued.

Mandela's preoccupation with the matter troubled me. If he was correct that the ANC had been 'under attack' and acted in self-defence, why had he and the hierarchy blocked the police investigation at every turn? And why had the minister misled the House? I asked him this exact question that day and he responded by telling us that, the night before the Shell House shootings, he had telephoned then President De Klerk and informed him of ANC intelligence reports that the marchers the next day were intending to target Shell House. 'De Klerk claimed he would inform the police chiefs, but they did nothing to prevent the march on our headquarters the next day,' he told us in a rather aggrieved fashion.

Later the following year, and just a few weeks after our May meeting in his office, Mandela took another swipe at me in the Senate; he charged that, as a consequence of our constant probing of Shell House, the DP had proved itself 'more right-wing than the National Party'.[11]

Irritated by the attention given to the Shell House Massacre, he reiterated later in the speech what he had told our parliamentary group in private, but now, in public for the first time, added that he personally had given the order to the guards to 'shoot to kill'.

Time, in the form of the December 1997 judicial inquest into Shell House, would prove Mandela wrong on the issue, and in May 1998 twelve ANC operatives applied for, and received, amnesty from the TRC for their role in the massacre.

In this and in many other judgment lapses, as I viewed them, Mandela's Teflon coating was ultra-resilient. The incident pointed to a central paradox in Madiba: he was capable of being the most partisan of politicians, but he was also the global-celebrity-cum-secular-saint, beyond politics. The 'thunderbolt of error' bounced right off him.

History, I suspect, will largely ignore these events or consign them to a footnote in the chapter on the run-up to election day – and the dawn of freedom – on 27 April. But I had thought the parliamentary skirmishing was noteworthy, since at the very commencement of democracy it was possible to believe that, even if the government's huge majority insulated it from procedural or substantive defeats, there was a strong feeling that the nation's legislature was opening up. This proved, over time, to be both brief and illusory.

The ask-no-questions-brook-no-dissent exile liberationists began to find the scrutiny to which they were now subjected a little too uncomfortable. This tendency would accelerate in future years. However, a central feature of the early Mandela presidency and the short-lived Government of National Unity – until 1996 – between the NP, the IFP and the ANC was the triangulated relationship between Mandela, De Klerk and Buthelezi. From the sidelines I became a fourth-man eyewitness to some of the events that troubled them in their forced, far from happy, marriage at the apex of power.

CHAPTER EIGHT

Forced Marriage

Brian Gilbertson, the angular, youthful-looking chief executive of the mining giant Gencor, was an unusual business titan in South Africa in the 1990s. More in desperation than expectation, I had visited him in about September 1995, to request funding for my party's very threadbare municipal election campaign. At the time, other than the Oppenheimer family, most of Johannesburg's commercial community met such entreaties with big smiles and very small, if any, cheques. Gilbertson, however, completely understood the need for robust opposition and promptly wrote a cheque for R250 000. He also requested my presence at the imminent opening of his company's corporate headquarters.

So rewarded, I presented myself on a balmy Friday evening in downtown Johannesburg at the rather splendidly reconfigured Gencor building. We were gathered, the leaders of South African corporate and political leadership, in a marquee set up outside.

I was not surprised by the presence of President Mandela, there to provide the keynote speech. After all, he set great store by obtaining the buy-in of business leaders, both to fund his cause and to keep faith with the course of the new South Africa. I had witnessed this just over a year before, in June 1994, at the banquet he hosted for François Mitterrand. I, along with other guests, had been somewhat startled, then, when he hastily departed the dinner after the first course. It later transpired that his finance minister (and Gilbertson's predecessor at Gencor), Derek Keys, was about to quit his post; Mandela needed to leave the dinner to telephone such business luminaries as Harry Oppenheimer, Donald Gordon and Marinus Daling to apprise them of this before it was announced, and to receive their blessing for his designated successor, Chris Liebenberg, the former head of Nedbank. Reassuring the markets and their leaders was a key presidential priority.

Equally unsurprising was the presence at the Gencor bash that evening of FW de Klerk. Gencor, after all, was the latest corporate iteration of General Mining, which, with some assistance from Anglo's Harry Oppenheimer, had in the mid-1960s become the first Afrikaner-controlled mining corporation in the country, nearly eighty years after gold had first been discovered on the Witwatersrand back in 1886. De Klerk was the inheritor of a patient political tradition that, in matters economic at least, set considerable store by the empowerment of *die volk* (the people, or Afrikaners).

But what followed was completely unexpected for the several hundred guests, me included, arrayed before the podium. Having commenced a prepared speech of suitable and forgettable politeness, Mandela took off his reading glasses midway through his courtesies and went vehemently off script. In altogether more memorable fashion, he launched a root-and-branch attack on the National Party, blaming it directly for the crime wave then engulfing the suburbs and townships of South Africa, and which had been a central theme of the recent local government elections in Johannesburg. His angry tone was reflected in his eyes, which seemed to focus directly on De Klerk, then serving alongside Mandela in the Government of National Unity (GNU). As the former president later wrote in his autobiography: 'He worded [the attack] in such a manner that it was clear that he had targeted me personally as leader of the party.'[1]

This somewhat dampened the bonhomie of the night, but we all duly retreated into the building for the banquet – all except Mandela, who had indicated he would have to leave before the meal began. It was only the next morning, when *The Star* newspaper splashed candid pictures across its pages, that South Africa learnt that Mandela's dressing-down of De Klerk had continued outside on the pavement. The photographs showed the two joint Nobel Prize winners wagging fingers at each other – with an anxious-looking Minister of Mineral and Energy Affairs, Pik Botha, trying to intercede. This was a further reminder to the country that the relationship at the summit of political power was neither peaceful nor happy. In fact, De Klerk and the National Party's presence in government would end, by their own hand, less than a year after the showdown that evening.

But, for the two years of their constitutional marriage in the GNU between 1994 and 1996, I was to receive first-hand testimony from the principals and their key lieutenants about the multiple causes of their unhappiness.

My first sighting of De Klerk after the elections of 1994 showed him to be in quite buoyant mood. Having just attacked me in parliament, he came over after the debate to 'wish me well' and to advise me that he was 'now firing on all cylinders'. Of course, while the DP was in occupation of a small sliver of the opposition benches, the NP, more than ten times larger than our party, uneasily straddled the divide between government and opposition. It could not very well launch strident attacks on the policy of a government of which it was a part. In addition, it was losing ground to the uninhibited DP, which, for all its other deficiencies, knew how to play an opposition role.

Parliament was often to witness the way in which the NP and its leader had become the 'punch bag of the new chamber'. This choice phrase was provided to me during a chat over tea in parliament with one of De Klerk's key lieutenants, Marthinus van Schalkwyk.

We were at that stage on friendly terms. Some six years later, he would collapse the diminishing party that De Klerk had bequeathed him into the newly formed Democratic Alliance, under my leadership. Neither he, nor our friendship, would survive this intensely unhappy union; Van Schalkwyk would ultimately leave De Klerk and his supporters and me behind when he accepted a post as an ANC cabinet minister.

But all that was very much in the future. On that day in the tea room, he bemoaned how the NP had to absorb all the sins of its past, for which there was 'no absolution'. The looming Truth and Reconciliation Commission (TRC), which opened the veritable Pandora's box of horrors the NP security apparatus had used to maintain its power, was, in the following years, to prove his assertion beyond contradiction. He told me, as well, that part of the problem in the new government was that

De Klerk's fellow NP ministers in the cabinet 'let him down and did not back him up'. Although De Klerk and I broadly emphasised the same points in debate – for instance, in support of free enterprise and skills redress coupled with the retention of competence – we were in truth broadly competing for the same constituency. In response to one or another of his attacks, I framed the position like this: 'His problem is less the credibility of his message than the lack of credibility of the messenger.'

Shortly thereafter, I attended yet another state banquet hosted by Mandela, this time for British Prime Minister John Major. I had by now become accustomed to the Mandela touch on these occasions, and we were spoilt for choice, since some sixty heads of state hotfooted it to South Africa during Mandela's presidency. About halfway through the dinner one of his aides would arrive at my table with the request, 'The president would like your presence.' I would then be escorted to the main table where a beaming Mandela would introduce me to the visiting head of state, always with the same introductory tag line: 'I want you to meet the leader of the Democratic Party – this young man gives me all my trouble!' He would then laugh heartily and offer some other compliments, before leaving me to engage in repartee with the foreign dignitary. So it was with Major and scores of other visiting grandees, from Pope John Paul II right down the moral scale to Zimbabwean President Robert Mugabe – not a special favourite of Mandela's and even less of mine.

This banter worked wonders for Mandela in displaying his style of inclusivity, and did no harm to my ego either. It did not, however, particularly charm Prince Philip, the Duke of Edinburgh, accompanying

Queen Elizabeth II on their historic visit to South Africa the following March, her first since 1947. At a small reception at the Cape Sun
Hotel before the formal dinner, Mandela repeated his usual introductory
line. The queen offered me a gloved hand to shake, but no comment.
Her more voluble consort, however, retorted, 'Why is your party called
"Democratic"? Aren't you all democrats now in South Africa?' He followed this with the observation, 'The problem with the word "democratic" is that all those republics in the Soviet Bloc called themselves
democratic and they weren't democratic at all, were they?' The prince, at
least, laughed at his own remarks.

But, on the night of the Major dinner, the invitation to me was delivered personally by De Klerk, who used the opportunity to buttonhole
me and suggest that it was 'high time we got together' for 'a chat, a coffee
or a whisky'. I had always had high regard for De Klerk's intelligence,
and admired him for his conspicuous displays of courage and steadfast-
ness. But I also realised that he could be very wily – a key complaint of
Mandela's – though perhaps this was a necessary quality for high-wire
power politics. Anyway, a meeting was scheduled for a few weeks hence.

Our relationship with the NP was uneasy and, at that stage, very uneven,
given that they vastly outnumbered us in parliament (eighty-three MPs
against seven). However, by the common accord of the media – affirmed, in
time, by voters – we were making the running as an opposition in contrast
to his party's performance. The NP had tried, with far less success than
Inkatha, to straddle its ambiguous role. I had also come to the conclusion
that a short-term route to re-establishing our relevance was to go after the
low-hanging fruit of disenchanted NP voters; the larger black constituency
was firmly with its liberators, the ANC. But the NP constituency was not

necessarily enjoying a rosy view of the current situation. De Klerk and half a dozen holdovers from his faded regime enjoyed high ministerial office under the new arrangements, but, as the UK chancellor of the exchequer said of the government of John Major after his dismissal from it, 'They were in office, but not in power.'

At our meeting in the Union Buildings in Pretoria, De Klerk was persuasive and plausible, if not formal. Like Buthelezi, he addressed me as 'Mr Leon' – in studied contrast to Mandela (and the rest of the country, come to think of it), who always called me 'Tony'. He informed me that our barbs against the NP in parliament and on the municipal election trail amounted to 'attacking the wrong target'. 'You should concentrate your fire on the ANC. They are the real enemy,' he counselled. De Klerk was, then, in favour of forming a joint caucus with the DP, to approach the finalisation of the new constitution (then being discussed by parliament sitting as a constitutional assembly) as a 'patriotic front' … a particularly unfortunate term, I thought at the time. I felt that such an idea would be a disaster, not simply because the appearance of ganging up would drive the ANC into a hardline or rejectionist stance (which it would have), but because it would diminish our influence on key issues.

I felt that separate but broadly converging approaches on essential matters would be more effective. In fact, the NP, now reduced from its previous monopoly of power to just over 20 per cent of the votes in the constitutional assembly, was to see few of the constitutional terms of trade move in its direction. The determination of the ANC not to renew, constitutionally, the power-sharing arrangements with the NP and others beyond 1999 would be the nail in the coffin of the NP's future place in government. I was more amenable to De Klerk's proposal that the opposition should – in his phrase – work together 'to cut the ANC down to size'. Yet when that unity was finally attained some years later with the launch of the Democratic Alliance, De Klerk had long retired from active politics and his party entered the new arrangement as the junior partner.

I sensed from that meeting that De Klerk, his formidable demeanour notwithstanding, was not much enjoying his role as second deputy president to Mandela, and that an essential acid had seeped into the chemistry of their personal relationship.

Some years after he had retired, De Klerk reflected with some feeling in his autobiography on his unhappiness in the new government. He wrote:

> Mandela never chose to involve me in any function outside the immediate role the constitution had determined for me [as one of two deputy presidents]. I was never asked to represent the country at international meetings or to carry out any other task of national importance. Neither did Mandela ever ask me to act as president during his frequent overseas visits. He always ensured that Thabo Mbeki remained in South Africa on such occasions to play this role.[2]

Personal slights aside, there was a structural design flaw in this coalition government. Elsewhere in the democratic world, such arrangements are occasioned by an election result in which no one party obtains an outright majority. South Africa's constitutional arrangement mandated a cabinet coalition, even though the majority party had obtained over 60 per cent of the votes. As De Klerk and others noted, this meant that the ANC could, and increasingly did, simply present its own policies to cabinet for approval and adamantly refused to negotiate or agree ground rules with its notional coalition partners (the NP and Inkatha) for a common policy approach. This much was kept behind cabinet doors at the time.

But at the end of the first year's parliamentary session, in late November 1994, I obtained a first-hand account of just how fraught the relationship had become, when I visited Mandela in his Pretoria residence. The ostensible purpose of this get-together, at which I was accompanied by some senior caucus colleagues, was to discuss something that De Klerk would describe pithily as '[t]he ANC style … of showing little respect to Parliament and even less to the opposition.'[3]

My frustrated caucus – who, despite our small number, were dealing with a myriad parliamentary committees and items of legislation in a malfunctioning parliament – had complained of serial delays and lack of quora at meetings, and other maladies afflicting the legislative process. I knew this from personal experience; our modest parliamentary presence meant that, in addition to being party leader, I also had to take on a direct parliamentary role as spokesman and member of the Portfolio Committee on Labour. Whatever incontestable improvements were wrought by the new democracy, efficiency was not much evident. And, despite some seriously impressive people in their vast parliamentary ranks, many ANC MPs – and certainly most members on my committee – seemed to regard parliament more as a tiresome inconvenience than a necessary focus of their attention. Chronic unpunctuality and absenteeism, without commensurate penalty, were, for example, some of the manifestations of this. Discussions with the Speaker and other senior office bearers in parliament had yielded no visible improvements.

I then suggested to my caucus that we avail ourselves of the open invitation that Mandela had given me to meet with him on any matter of concern, and that we discuss some of these challenges directly with the head of state.

'Colin,' Mandela said, turning to our veteran parliamentary caucus chairman, Colin Eglin, 'you sit at the head of the table – you are the senior man here in terms of service.' So advised, Eglin, first elected to parliament some thirty-six years before, in 1958, and the rest of our group arranged ourselves around the dining room table at Libertas, as the president's Pretoria residence was known at the time, and we all sat down to a lunch of soup, lasagne and fruit.

In the light of the fact that our purpose was to discuss with Mandela the inefficiencies of the legislature, we had embarrassingly undercut our case by arriving ten minutes late: a miscommunication had directed us first to Mandela's office in the Union Buildings. He waved away our apologies and mocked teasingly, 'At last I have something to criticise you about!' Given both his age and the fact that Mandela had only returned that morning from a visit to Morocco, he seemed highly engaged and very relaxed, dressed in one of his by-now-famous batik-style shirts. When I so commented, he riposted, 'One of the advantages of presidential life is that the plane comes equipped with a bed.'

A crisp suggestion of ours was that the duties of the minister in charge of government business in parliament be transferred from Trade and Industry Minister Trevor Manuel. We had considerable regard for Manuel's ministerial competence, but these seemed to distract him from the needs and the minutiae of parliamentary matters. We suggested that Water Affairs Minister Kader Asmal, whose ministry was less burdensome but whose enjoyment of parliament was considerable, might make an appropriate choice.

Mandela dismissed our proposal out of hand, saying, 'Kader has great ability but he talks too much.' There was an interesting aspect to his appraisal of Asmal (and indeed there was no topic on which he did not express himself). Mandela and Walter Sisulu had persuaded Asmal ('against my better judgment', he later told me) to stand against Thabo Mbeki for the position of party chairman in 1993, when the position became vacant after the death of Oliver Tambo. This was apparently more on the grounds of his Indian ethnicity than in recognition of his talents, in order to ensure that the ANC embodied its own 'non-racial' credentials. He was crushed by Mbeki in the ensuing vote of the party's National Executive Committee.

Matters of loquacity led Mandela into a complaint about De Klerk. He told us that he had recently called his deputy out of a cabinet meeting and told him that 'he should not speak on every item on the cabinet agenda'. According to Mandela, De Klerk had responded to this entreaty by complaining that, since Pik Botha and Roelf Meyer (two of his key NP ministers) kept quiet, he had to do 'all the talking for his side'. This essentially tallied with Van Schalkwyk's complaint to me a few months earlier. Mandela archly informed us that 'De Klerk has not reconciled himself with his loss of power'.

Of more general, and I thought persuasive, interest was how Mandela, perhaps disarmingly, described that day the ANC's transition from struggle to power without having had the benefit of any intervening preparation. Whatever his dislike for the Nationalists and their current leader, he had clearly studied the organisation quite closely. When, during the lunch, Colin Eglin and Ken Andrew (then chairman of the parliamentary Standing Committee on Public Accounts) presented some specific problems experienced in the new parliament and suggested solutions, Mandela, after listening intently, responded: 'The ANC went straight from the bush into power.' He reminded us that the most significant previous regime change in twentieth-century South Africa had been the ousting of the United Party government in 1948 by the National Party. But, Mandela noted, the NP 'had served a long period in opposition in parliament before assuming power'. The implication here was obvious: denied the same learning curve, the ANC could hardly be expected to conform to our idea of efficient parliamentary government.

At a previous meeting with Mandela, I had been surprised when he told me how much he respected De Klerk's predecessor, PW Botha. 'At least you knew where you stood with him', he had said, laughing. I was even more surprised when he revealed that he sometimes enjoyed telephone conversations with the apartheid strongman and reluctant reformer, known as *die groot krokodil* (the big crocodile), then living in grumpy retirement in the southern Cape seaside town named – appropriately perhaps – Wilderness. But such amity clearly did not prevail with Botha's successor.

Within weeks of our Pretoria lunch with the president, matters between Mandela and De Klerk would spiral out of control, and into the open. Some nine months before their verbal brawl on the pavement outside Gencor, South Africa saw direct evidence of a political marriage in deep crisis.

Mandela clearly did not hide from outsiders his irritation with De Klerk. He had also informed the world that his lack of trust, clashing vanities aside, stemmed from his belief that, if not directly complicit, De Klerk was at best negligent in failing to heed or check the activities of the 'third force', or security force machine, which had fomented township violence and killings, mostly against supporters of the ANC, during the rocky years of transition.

De Klerk's understandable frustration and difficulty – combining an executive post in cabinet and an opposition role outside it – collided with Mandela's lack of trust at an explosive cabinet meeting in late January 1995.

In Mandela's version, as related by his authorised biographer Anthony Sampson, the dam wall burst when Mandela discovered that just before the election 3 500 policemen had been granted indemnity from prosecution for crimes committed during the apartheid years. According to Sampson, in front of the cabinet:

> [Mandela] launched into a tirade about De Klerk's underhand amnesty and disloyalty to the coalition government. He praised other Afrikaner Ministers, including Roelf Meyer and Pik Botha, concentrating his abuse on De Klerk. 'It was a bristling attack,' said one observer, 'but with paragraphs and sentences perfectly constructed.' De Klerk started putting away his papers, and said he must reconsider his position.[4]

According to De Klerk's version, the proximate cause of this explosion, and his response, was, in fact, a strategy at the cabinet meeting devised by several ANC ministers to 'call [him] to account' for public attacks on the ANC. De Klerk defended himself, stating that he was within his rights 'to criticise and oppose decisions that had been taken by the government despite our opposition to them in cabinet'.[5] This, of course, went to the heart of the structural fault in the government's make-up.

De Klerk also wrote that Mandela only joined the debate and introduced the indemnity issue when 'it seemed that ANC ministers had been swayed by my arguments'.[6] Mandela intervened by saying that 'he would not let me get away with my debating abilities'. Mandela added sundry other charges to his list of complaints against De Klerk, all of which, in De Klerk's version, lacked any substantiation. 'By the end of Mandela's tirade I was furious ... and said that the National Party members of the cabinet were going to withdraw [from the cabinet meeting] ... to reconsider our continued participation in the government ...'[7]

Almost immediately, the row entered the public domain, dipping the stock market and depressing the currency, with the prospect of the second party of government ceasing to be part of it. The very next evening at an NP Congress, De Klerk confirmed to the world that in view of the severity of the attack on him, he was 'seriously thinking' of withdrawal.

But, in the best Mandela and more recent South African tradition, a photo opportunity and a handshake was arranged the next day between the two antagonists. Mutual expressions of 'good faith and integrity' were proffered, and the immediate crisis was averted. Although De Klerk insisted to Mandela that his continuation in government could not be contingent on 'a smile and a handshake' and that proper written ground rules were now required to clarify the role of being a member of government and opposition, these were never forthcoming. Several arguments and eighteen months later, De Klerk and the NP exited the government forever.

Whatever sensitivity or sense of history Mandela believed De Klerk lacked, there were, in my own considerably more harmonious relationship with Mandela with its less frequent encounters, two less attractive attributes that De Klerk identified in the ANC leader, which I, too, would sometimes experience: '[H]is habit of flying off the handle without properly c hecking his facts beforehand; and secondly his tactic of papering over problems with charm and promises, without taking effective remedial action.'[8]

De Klerk was also nothing if not brutally realistic in assessing this period: 'We had been forced together to legitimize the new South Africa. Now the honeymoon was over.'[9]

During an agreeable get-together many years later – in the week, in fact, of Mandela's death in December 2013 – I received an interesting observation from one of Mandela's key cabinet lieutenants from that time. He did not believe Mandela had treated De Klerk properly at all times in the course of their cohabitation at the heart of government, but 'not because of De Klerk himself'. My ANC friend explained: 'In Mandela's eyes, De Klerk became the proxy for much of the anger he felt, and managed so masterfully to mask from view, towards the group and community FW came from.'

The Chief

THERE WAS A third party in the 'forced marriage' that created the multiparty Government of National Unity presiding over South Africa's democratic transition: Prince Mangosuthu Gatsha Buthelezi.

I grew up in Durban and had a precocious interest in politics. As such, Buthelezi, the chief minister of the homeland of KwaZulu – a friend of my father, and an admired figure in our household – was prominent in my budding political consciousness. Better than any of his homeland colleagues, Buthelezi appeared to succeed in maintaining hostility to Pretoria's grand apartheid design while using the 'Bantustan' platform it provided to develop a political base of size and influence. Of course, his emphasis on peaceful negotiations, a market economy and federalism appealed to the small community of liberal whites.

On the other side of the political divide, his relationship with the ANC, of which he had once been a member, had, during its long years of prohibition and exile, plummeted. He was seen variously as a sell-out and as a ruthless opportunist. His erratic behaviour during the constitutional negotiations and his alignment with a grab bag of right-wing forces cemented this image.

But it was the civil war between Buthelezi's Inkatha movement (which later became the Inkatha Freedom Party) and the ANC – the two vying for ascendancy in Natal and on the Witwatersrand – that poisoned their relationship even further in the period leading to the 1994 election. Alone, Buthelezi's Inkatha Freedom Party (IFP) could, certainly in Natal, challenge the ANC monopoly on black support, and the election result that recorded an outright majority for the IFP in the province had proved this. Their emphatic win on my home ground also catapulted Buthelezi and two others into the cabinet alongside Mandela and De Klerk.

Prior to the election, my only contact with him had been a single and inconclusive meeting during the constitutional negotiations at which I found his diffidence, even awkwardness, to be at variance with his public image of truculence.

But, early in the life of the new parliament and spurred by Mandela's clear preoccupation with him, I sought a more substantive discussion with the Zulu prince. I also knew that, in contrast with the situation with De Klerk's NP, there was no overlap between our respective constituencies, and thus less in-built competition between our parties. Further, on paper at least, our policies had much in common.

Buthelezi's new perch as Minister of Home Affairs had secured him a suite of offices in the – for the times – ironically named HF Verwoerd Building (soon renamed), an appropriately grim edifice directly opposite the Houses of Parliament, where the government was accommodated. It was there that we met. He was exquisitely polite and etiquette weighed heavily upon him.

I was a little nonplussed when he drew a sheaf of papers from his pocket and proceeded to read to me, an audience of one, what essentially amounted to a speech. In his discourse, he noted the many unfulfilled promises that had been made to him prior to the election, and that he had accepted his ministry and service in the government 'only because of intense pressure from the IFP national council'. I was too polite to comment that, in a party he so comprehensively dominated, this might seem slightly exaggerated. He did not offer any direct opinion of Mandela, but did observe that his presence in the national unity arrangements made him 'uncomfortable'.

He considerably lightened up, however, when I suggested that both our parties should seek common ground where possible. This set the stage for events, many meetings and years later, when the two parties entered into a formal coalition in the KwaZulu-Natal legislature in 2003. However, our national arrangement in the election the following year, which we dubbed a 'coalition for change', proved disappointing.

His 1994 'discomfort' was given prime-time coverage in the bizarre appearance he made on South African television some months after our first meeting. One Sunday evening in late September that year, millions of viewers were presented with the startling sight of the minister tussling on air with Prince Sifiso Zulu, a spokesman of the Zulu king, Zwelithini. Apparently, Buthelezi had been in an interview in an adjoining studio and had stormed into the interview with Sifiso, who was explaining the king's decision the week before to break ties with Buthelezi. In the course of the on-air altercation a gun was produced,[1] though no shot was fired. The king's allegiance, hitherto with his cousin Buthelezi, was a prize totem in the struggle between the IFP and ANC for the support of his subjects. Scenting the definite change in the political weather, the king was now going with the national ruling party, hence Buthelezi's on-camera rage.[2]

Sifiso Zulu would become infamous in the years ahead, and for reasons far more serious than his TV joust with Buthelezi. In 2010, he was sentenced to three years in jail for culpable homicide after killing two people and injuring eight others, in a collision in Durban when, drunk behind the wheel, he had jumped a red light in his luxury BMW. He served just under a third of the sentence. He made headlines before his trial when he attempted to commit suicide, and, apparently as a consequence of his royal and ANC links, his high living became the stuff of legend in my home town of Durban.

At the time of the spat, Mandela himself was apparently resting at a health hydro in Stellenbosch. The TV debacle forced his early return to office to attempt to patch up the quarrel.

The always-ambivalent relationship between Madiba and Buthelezi began to fray even further thereafter. A promissory note thrown by Mandela and De Klerk at Inkatha during the helter-skelter arrangements preceding the 1994 election – promising 'international mediation' on issues such as the degree of federal autonomy – had not been honoured by the ANC. As a consequence, Inkatha boycotted the Constitutional Assembly, and the political temperature – never particularly low in the province of KwaZulu-Natal – glared red.

In a May Day speech, delivered in the populous and poverty-stricken township of Umlazi south of Durban in 1995, Mandela lost control and blamed Inkatha for the upsurge of violence in the province. In bare-knuckled fashion, he told his audience that he would 'cut off the funds to the province' – a blatantly unconstitutional threat. These provocative remarks were in response to Buthelezi (termed by Mandela 'a certain leader in KwaZulu-Natal'), who, in a speech at the same venue, announced, as Mandela saw it, that 'he would organise people to revolt against the government'. Mandela warned: '[Those] who call on Zulus to resist the authority of Pretoria don't know what they have started. Those responsible for violence will be dealt with.'[3]

The very next day, 2 May, was a marquee event in parliament – the president's own budget vote. As I grappled with preparing my own speech for that afternoon's debate, I received a call from Mandela. He requested me to forgo my speaking turn until he had had an opportunity to brief me personally on the situation in KwaZulu-Natal. I explained to him that, if I were to accede, I would be knocked out of the debate until the following day, rendering my contribution largely pointless. I also sensed that, after a private briefing from the president, my guns would effectively be spiked.

Mandela then suggested we meet after the debate. I agreed, and used the talk to implore him to meet the IFP's demand for mediation, however eccentric and moot it now might appear. As the private dialogue flowed to and fro, the president interrupted me with a personal and unmerited compliment ('You are a brilliant young man') and a warning: 'The matter is essentially political and my patience with Buthelezi is now exhausted.'

The debate was strange. Mandela never once referred to the storm that had erupted over his KwaZulu-Natal speech, while Buthelezi went for the jugular, directly referring to the president's 'threats' and launching a lengthy justification of his own position. He quoted himself as saying that South Africa and KwaZulu-Natal must rise and resist the central government 'which has given a clear indication of pressing plans from which great evil arises'.[4] Jeers from the ANC benches punctuated his presentation.

For my part, I told parliament I was shocked and saddened by the events in Umlazi – 'a vivid example of the gross vein of political intolerance and violence which is still alive in our country'. Here I had in mind the fact that apparently several hundred IFP supporters had tried to storm Mandela's rally and allegedly shot and injured several people inside the stadium. I said that, in my party's 'objective view', international mediation should continue, even on the terms of reference agreed to thirteen months earlier, which had themselves now become a source of disputation. I suggested less confrontation.

When I later met Mandela (with Colin Eglin, who the president suggested accompany me), he appeared perfectly calm, though determined. He elaborated on the violence and intimidation meted out to his supporters throughout KwaZulu-Natal – although nothing seemed to justify the threat of turning off the taps to the province. I was also rather surprised when Mandela suggested that I obtain the views of my 'security people' on the situation in the troubled province. I did not want to disillusion the president in his estimation of my resources party's and priorities, by indicating there was no such apparatus inside the DP. However, given his own background and the prevailing structures in the ANC, it was clear that 'security' was a key element of the ruling party's structures and informed the decision-making of the party and of its president.

In his reply to the debate, Mandela drew a clear line between the precepts of the constitution and the necessity of saving human life:

> I do not believe the constitution to be more important than human lives ... [The] constitution is very important, and it is a matter of serious concern when the president of a country threatens to change the constitution, but I am determined to protect human life. The perception that whites in this country do not care about black lives is there. I may not share it but it is there. The discussions [during this debate in parliament] where reference is not even made to the principal reason for my having taken this tough line to protect human lives, unfortunately goes a long way in confirming this perception.[5]

The immediate crisis passed. The threats and counter-threats lessened. There was, however, no mediation – but also no cut-off of funds. Thereafter, Mandela's method of dealing with Buthelezi went from cajoling to charm. He repeatedly appointed Buthelezi as acting president when both he and Mbeki were out of South Africa (a frequent occurrence). If Buthelezi was not entirely mollified, his continuance in the GNU was ensured.

Whether by design or not, it was during one of these interludes, in September 1998, that Acting President Buthelezi stunned the country and the world by announcing that he had authorised the SA National Defence Force's entry into Lesotho to 'restore democracy' there. As one of the opposition leaders in parliament, I was summoned by Buthelezi to a meeting, in terms of the constitution, to be apprised of the justification for the announcement of the 'invasion'. I found Buthelezi's briefing both hesitant and unpersuasive, and told him that South Africa had not exhausted all peaceful avenues to resolve the crisis in Maseru. He took extreme umbrage at my remark (not always a difficult posture for him, but rare in our interactions to date) and a chill entered our relations for a while afterward.

An interesting sidenote to this was how Mandela would later describe the botched (in execution) invasion of our tiny neighbouring state as 'an intervention to restore democracy and the rule of law'.[6] Some years later, in January 2003, Mandela would join the worldwide condemnation of President George W Bush's pre-emptive invasion of Iraq, although the US president cited some of the same grounds for his actions as Mandela had used about Lesotho. Party colleague (and Bush admirer) Jack Bloom described Mandela's ex post facto justification for Lesotho as 'pure Bush doctrine three years before Bush himself had enunciated it'.[7]

Buthelezi was to outlast Mandela and De Klerk in government by many years. When I retired from party leadership in 2007 and quit parliament two years later, he still remained, in his 80s, at his parliamentary and leadership posts – though, by then, without cabinet status, and presiding over a party in the steepest decline.

It was, in fact, in dealing with two personalities far closer to me, personally and politically, than either Buthelezi or De Klerk, that led to one of the more surreal of my interactions with Mandela, and provided a further insight into his presidential style.

CHAPTER TEN

Trading Liberals

THE SMALL SWISS town of Carouge, just outside Geneva, was the unlikely setting for one of the stranger interludes in my interactions with Mandela. Back in March 1995, it was in a small pension in this village, the home of my stepbrother, Alan Downing, that my father had gathered his family to celebrate his seventieth birthday. Carouge, with its neatness and impeccable order, and just a hint of the avant-garde in its high-end bars and boutiques, is a postcard-perfect market town that effortlessly symbolises Switzerland's status as the epicentre of the First World. It was about as far as you could get from the heat and dust of home.

But it was there, just before breakfast one morning, that I was interrupted by the manager's shouting in an excitable and, to my ears, indecipherable French something along the lines of '*le téléphone*' and '*le président*'.

I made my way to the hostelry's sole public telephone and was astonished to discover it was none other than Mandela's secretary on the line.

She had tracked me down from Mozambique, where Mandela was visiting and perhaps courting his future wife, Graça, widow of the country's late President Samora Machel, who lived in the capital, Maputo. The secretary advised me the president needed to speak to me urgently. I had no idea what had caused the latest crisis.

When he came on the line, he told me 'we' needed to resolve swiftly a problem relating to the DP's proposal to nominate Professor John Dugard to the soon-to-be-established Human Rights Commission (HRC). While government had the 'highest regard' for Professor Dugard, they felt it was necessary for Helen Suzman to add her expertise and stature to the new body. He was 'certain that the DP would want to support her', as he beguilingly put it.

I was caught completely off-guard and felt deeply conflicted.

First, there were the personalities involved. My relationship with Suzman stretched back decades to when I first became an activist in the political cause that, for thirteen years, she represented alone in parliament. Although we had become close, my successful effort to replace her as MP for Houghton in 1989 had frustrated her plans for the succession to pass to her cousin and long-time colleague, Irene Menell. At the time of Mandela's call, the breach had not been healed. Doubtless this explained why her decision to place her name in nomination for the HRC had bypassed the party. But, at the dawn of democracy, it seemed a body of some significance. Under Chapter 9 of the constitution, it was charged with 'promoting respect for human rights' and their promotion, protection and attainment. While nominations to the body were recommended by parliament, the president was empowered to make the final appointments.

John Dugard was a horse of a very different colour. I had been first a student of his at the University of Witwatersrand and later a colleague, when I lectured there. Like generations of law students and academics, I knew that Dugard's pioneering work in promoting a human rights discourse in South Africa, long before the constitution had been enacted, was both singular and brave.

After Dugard's excellently merited nomination to the Constitutional Court had been rejected the previous year, my parliamentary colleagues and I felt acutely that this man, a bright light during the long apartheid night, would be a worthy commissioner. We had accordingly strongly motivated his candidacy. However, Mandela made it clear in the course of our intercontinental conversation that it would be 'disproportionate' (or words to that effect) for the liberal/DP camp to have more than one nominee – and he required me to choose. I had not been aware that Suzman had sought, or received, nomination, but I immediately realised how politically and personally perilous it would be for me and the party to be seen not to support her.

I was appalled at the prospect of Dugard being dropped again, and mortified that I was being railroaded into exercising a choice – which I made in favour of Suzman. (I did think she, too, justified inclusion.) I never discerned why the government was so resolute on not appointing Dugard, who was hardly a DP partisan, as Suzman was. It might have been those racial, gender or quota-filling requirements that soon – on an ever-accelerating basis – became the *raison d'être* for all public appointments. Or perhaps senior ANC figures bore some personal animus towards the distinguished and mild-mannered professor. The mystery has never been explained, and Dugard was to be a double casualty of the democratic transition to which he had so resolutely dedicated himself.

I found both the call and the choice Mandela presented me with that morning intensely discomforting. It suggested, and this later became the iron rule in the new South Africa, just as it had pervaded the old republic, that individual merit would be placed second to racial and po-litical preferment. That the liberal community would, almost by defini-tion, have more rights activists in its camp as a proportion of its overall numerical strength was passed over in this early signal that political and racial representivity would trump other considerations.

Doubtless, Mandela also wanted to use his powers to reward his friends. In the case of Suzman, her visits to Robben Island during the grimmest years of his incarceration there and her fight to improve conditions for political prisoners had created an infrangible bond with Mandela. In any event her staunch fight for human rights under apartheid made her an excellent choice, whatever my misgivings about Dugard's exclusion. But she was part of a large army of people, some of lesser merit, who Mandela believed should have some stardust sprinkled on them during his tenure. As Anthony Sampson explained it, '[h]e relished his person-al patronage, offering old friends grand jobs like ambassadorships and watching their surprise'.[1]

His preferment of some of these 'old friends' at home and abroad would, over time, tarnish other aspects of Mandela's vision for democracy and human rights.

But his appointments to the HRC, incidental as they were to the larger canvas he was painting at the time, did have some deeper consequences that would endure long after the first commission had been inaugurated.

They would also provide some early signals on the future direction of the country and the bitter nature of its public discourse.

The first of these concerned another close friend, the legal luminary – later High Court judge – Dennis Davis. Davis was a protean intellect and was remarkably adept at straddling many disciplines and differing ideologies on the liberal-left spectrum. But few in the old, or new, order could match his impeccable non-racial credentials and his fierce detestation of the recently vanquished apartheid schema. This made his objection to Dugard's exclusion from the HRC – and the means used by its new chairman to counter him – very instructive and profoundly troubling.

It all exploded publicly, on television, about a year after my Swiss conversation with the president.

In an article he wrote a few weeks before his debate with HRC chairman, Professor Barney Pityana, Davis had objected to certain of the new members (not Suzman) appointed to the body. In singling out Dugard's exclusion, Davis went on to note: "'The commission appeared to be perceived as a useful avenue to reward a number of its appointees for services rendered. In the case of a couple of appointees, their knowledge of human rights was conspicuous only by its absence.'"[2]

An infuriated Pityana had written back 'that "Davis and his ilk are racists" since they could not accept a commission appointed ultimately by an elected black president'.[3]

In the subsequent debate, Pityana took his mind-blocking response further by noting that the singling out of Dugard was because he was white. Davis, in response, described himself as being saddened that his criticism "'marks me as a racist'", and called on Pityana to resign as chairman.[4]

Pityana did not heed the advice and the commission ploughed on under his baton in controversial, often administratively chaotic, circumstances; it achieved some further infamy in conducting an audit of 'racism in the news media', among other delights. Suzman resigned from the commission before her term expired and complained bitterly about Pityana's performance as its chairman.

Relating to this early sign of how legitimate and well-merited criticism of public appointments would be met, a wider point was very well described shortly before this spat by a friend of both Davis's and mine, the towering liberal legal academic Etienne Mureinik. He wrote, in respect of another full-blown race row in 1995 at the University of Witwatersrand about the fitness for office of Professor William Makgoba, of the 'strength of naked uncritical race solidarity'. With great foresight, given the momentum this strategy would achieve in the years ahead, he prophesied: 'It [undermines] the hope of a society in which white leaders can call a black leader to account under criteria equally binding on all … [and it destroys] any hope of equal accountability.'[5]

Within months of writing those fateful words, in July 1996 Etienne would commit suicide at the age of just 42. His death both shocked and intensely saddened his many friends and colleagues, in whose ranks I was proud to be counted. However, I was determined to use my opposition post to press on for 'full accountability', regardless of his warning and my lack of pigment.

But I would fairly shortly afterwards receive a tempting invitation that offered to change the relationship between the president and his pesky opponents fundamentally.

CHAPTER ELEVEN

The Temptation

DUST AND GRIT swirled into the summer air as the large SA Air Force helicopter settled gingerly on the parched arena of Sharpeville's George Thabe Stadium, a venue more readily associated with the ups and downs of township soccer rivalry.

This occasion, though, was very different. Once the dust had cleared, I, and no doubt many others among the thousands in the packed stands, watched with a keen awareness of the historic conjunction of the moment as Nelson Mandela emerged from the side door of the aircraft to clamorous applause. Seldom had guest of honour, venue and date been so perfectly fused as they were that day in 1996 near the banks of the Vaal River, the boundary between the provinces of Gauteng and Free State.

It was on this International Human Rights Day, 10 December 1996, that Mandela would sign the new constitution into law at a place that weighed heavy with the conflicted national history, away from which this testament could now perhaps provide a path, into a future undergirded by freedom and democracy. For it was at Sharpeville some thirty-six years before, on 21 March 1960, that police had shot and killed sixty-nine black people engaged in an anti-pass law demonstration, a protest against the document every black South African was legally obliged to carry, to be vouched for in so-called white South Africa.

Although the Sharpeville protest was organised by the Pan Africanist Congress, rivals of the ANC, it was the tipping point that galvanised, and radicalised, mass black resistance to the apartheid order. A more distant historical echo resonated on that day in 1996; not far from the George Thabe Stadium is the site of the signing of the Treaty of Vereeniging, which ended hostilities between the British and the Boer republics in 1902. It was a peace that sealed the disenfranchisement of black people and ushered in a politics that laid the foundations of apartheid.

Signing the new constitution, which Mandela did a short while after his arrival at the stadium, was the symbolic and substantive moment, in the two years since democracy finally swept onto these southern shores, of the inking of a new and more hopeful chapter in the country's history.

After the signing ceremony and speeches by Mandela, appropriately flanked by some veteran survivors of the Sharpeville massacre, and Constitutional Assembly chairman Cyril Ramaphosa, I joined throngs of other guests in the marquee for refreshments. I literally bumped into the president there, and took the opportunity to mention that I hoped he had received my invitation to a far lesser event some five days hence, the celebration of my 40th birthday. Mandela seemed genuinely puzzled that he had no information about my birthday bash, which I had hardly expected him to. But he promised to do his best to attend.

On Sunday 15 December at the Houghton home of my friends Cliff and Robyn Garrun – on which I depended to accommodate the numbers, my cottage being too small for the purpose – the great man duly arrived, sprinkling some magic dust on the star-struck guests, many of whom were social friends whose lives were untouched by politics and the personalities starring on its stage. Mangosuthu Buthelezi was also present, and both made warm speeches, much to the delight of my parents.

On taking his leave, Mandela wished me a happy festive season, adding, casually I thought, 'We must talk in the New Year.' I thought nothing further of the significance, if any, of this remark, and proceeded to leave behind the cares of politics for a trip to a game reserve.

But there had been meaning in Mandela's seemingly offhand remark. It all became public some weeks hence. In Cape Town, for instance, motorists driving home on 23 January 1997 must have been surprised to see the *Cape Argus* billboards speculating 'Tony Leon for the Cabinet?' They would not, however, have been as surprised as I had been a week earlier. My enjoyment of the prospect of a *tête-à-tête* with Mandela – requested by him through his secretary, Mary Mxadana – had been offset to an extent by her insistence that I present myself at his Houghton home for breakfast at 6am. Early rising was an ingrained habit of Mandela (who, as I knew, was an old-school practitioner of the 'early to bed, early to rise' tradition), but my body clock worked in the opposite direction.

Nevertheless, a presidential summons required punctuality, and, after making my way through a thicket of security personnel, I found the president on his doorstep, needlessly apologetic for the early-morning scheduling necessitated by his having to leave at 7.30 for an ANC *lekgotla*.

We sat down to a breakfast far more sumptuous – fruit, porridge, eggs, fish and coffee – than my constitution could tolerate at that hour. Towards the end of the meal Mandela let loose his thunderbolt: 'Would you consider joining me in the cabinet and helping to strengthen governance?' I was blindsided, and could think of no appropriate response, except to thank him and ask for time to consider the implications.

I did have the presence of mind at the time to use an item, currently in the news, as an indicator of how Mandela and the government were dealing with a controversial issue, and whether any putative DP presence in the cabinet could be remotely compatible with an opposition perspective. South Africa was set to sell R3 billion worth of tank-firing systems to Syria. The cabinet committee charged with ensuring that we did not export ordnance to rights-delinquent regimes or high-conflict areas was chaired by Kader Asmal. Had his attention been elsewhere? The ruthless Ba'athist regime of President Hafez al-Assad, and the potential abyss of Middle East conflict, should have immediately spiked the suggestion.

Mandela became extremely agitated; he told me the matter was far from concluded, but that he was 'infuriated' by America's reported response to the deal. He then launched 'the struggle defence' – he said he and the ANC looked at the world as being divided between countries that fought against apartheid ('which was criminal and lacked any respect for human rights') and those that supported it. Hence, Syria was pro-ANC and America pro-apartheid. I countered by pointing out that, for at least the last two decades of apartheid, most of the West prohibited arms sales to South Africa – and, whatever role Syria played in support of the ANC at the time, I thought it ill behoved our country to embrace and arm its regime. On the matter of Syria, at least from the vantage point of this writing in 2013, it would appear that future events would bear out my warning, more than Mandela's indignation that morning. Our breakfast time ran out.

I immediately set in process a series of discussions with trusted colleagues about whether, in principle, we should explore the matter further. I was equally determined not to leak any suggestion or hint of the offer to the media, realising that, apart from the gross discourtesy to Mandela that this would involve, the feeding frenzy of speculation would impair a proper and sober evaluation. However, 'a source in the Presidency' (for which Mandela apologised, by phone, on the evening of our early-morning meeting) was not as restrained. Within a day or two it was all the stuff of headlines.

My only public comment was diplomatic: 'It would have been churlish not to have taken into account Mandela's hand of friendship,' I told *The Sowetan*.[1] They informed their readers that the 'DP's participation in the GNU seems a foregone conclusion'.

However, Mandela was not our only political suitor. The day before my early-morning meeting, I had a call from FW de Klerk, the leader of the opposition – which he had become after his exit from the GNU. The NP was also seeking our hand, and four days hence he would be announcing a 'new initiative' possibly leading to a new party to contest the next election. He was sure, he added, that the DP, IFP and NP held enough 'common values' to enthuse millions of voters who currently supported parties more for reasons of history than for current reality. He urged me 'not to shoot down the idea'. I gave him the assurance he sought.

The Mandela offer was generally welcomed by the party; De Klerk's new initiative was not. I also sought an early meeting with Buthelezi – who seemed, after three years, to have adroitly straddled the conflicting demands of government and opposition. The minuscule PAC and its diminutive new leader, former bishop Stanley Mogoba, also came into play. Mogoba is a person of great warmth and naiveté, to whom Mandela's offer had also been extended. Buthelezi told me (and Douglas Gibson and DP KwaZulu-Natal leader, Roger Burrows) in late January that, should the PAC accept Mandela's offer, and we reject it, prospects of racial polarisation would increase, with three essentially black parties in government arraigned against mostly white parties outside. He said the DP joining would be 'a good thing'.

Amid public speculation and private soundings I oscillated: was it a golden chance or a poisoned chalice? In the midst of my uncertainty, I bumped into senior Anglo executive Leslie Boyd and sought his counsel. 'Following your gut instinct is always the best way to resolve a finely balanced question,' he wisely advised.

'But, Les,' I responded, 'the problem is that my gut keeps changing on this matter.'

'In that case,' he said, 'follow your first one.' This was no doubt sound, but all I could remember was deep ambivalence.

Harry Oppenheimer and Bobby Godsell believed we should 'give it a go'. However, when I bumped into Van Zyl Slabbert at a cricket match, he urged me to stay out. Helen Suzman did not wait for me to contact her, and warned me, via the press, that 'it would be a big mistake' and one 'sorely disappointing to hardcore DP supporters'.[2]

But Suzman was not the only person going public on the issue. An 'unnamed government source', quoted by *The Mercury*, informed its readers (and me) that I would be offered the post of Minister of Public Enterprises.[3] Here, I thought, would be the rock on which my party and the government would wreck our incipient relationship. An ardent privatisation zealot sent into a department of statist officials? A poacher turned gamekeeper indeed.

My unease intensified when I reread Mandela's 8 January statement on his party's expanded and expansive view on the role of 'the cadre': these appropriately Leninist figures were to be deployed everywhere … 'in places of residence, in schools, places of worship, in the workplace, on the sports fields, in government, in the legislatures'. They should be neither 'political' nor ANC simply 'after hours'.[4] I envisaged myself as a minister atop a department stuffed full of ANC apparatchiks, answerable and unswervingly loyal to the party of which I was most decidedly not a member. Incidentally, here was the first formalisation of the policy of 'cadre deployment' and the seizure of the state by the party faithful that would so impede South Africa's future path to deepening democracy and economic growth.

Still, I was sincere when I told *The Citizen* that 'an offer to join a government has to be taken very seriously. It's not something I would dismiss out of hand, but it's not something I would accept without qualification and very serious thought.'[5]

While my office was negotiating a time to obtain some specificity around his proposal, I received a phone call from a casualty of De Klerk's previous government, the former health minister, Dr Rina Venter. Venter, who would soon join the DP, warned me that the biggest mistake De Klerk had made – which doomed his ill-starred role in the GNU – was his inability, at any stage, to pin down Mandela as to the precise ground rules for minority parties in the coalition government. The essence of the issue was to obtain, explicitly, a manner enabling the DP to distance itself publicly from policies agreed to in cabinet with which it fundamentally dissented.

If De Klerk, with six colleagues to back him up and whose membership of Mandela's government was mandated by the constitution, could not achieve such an agreement, how could I hope to succeed?

During the annual State of the Nation debate in February, I told parliament what I really thought: 'South Africa is governed by an administration with a clashing agenda of competing and contradictory priorities; a ship of state which sails without a moral compass and a government of hindsight, not foresight. The ANC reminds me of priests who have kept their faith but lost their religion ... I see a revolutionary movement, which stood for perhaps the greatest universal good in the second half of the twentieth century – the eradication of racism and the elimination of apartheid – now practising so many instances of new racism.'[6]

Such admonitions did not seem to trouble the ANC. Indeed, one of its more thoughtful members, Willie Hofmeyr, soon to exit parliament to head up one of the country's anti-corruption arms, wrote perceptively: 'A decision by the DP to join the GNU will bring little direct benefit to the ANC, but is primarily based on the interests of the country.'[7]

I finally met once more with Mandela on this matter in Pretoria towards the end of February, just two days before the DP's Federal Council was to meet in Durban. Mandela pointed out that there were often vehement disagreements in cabinet, and members were free to express their viewpoint. 'But what if we wish to go public with our dissent?' I asked the president.

His immediate answer sealed the matter for me: 'We must go out and face the world with one voice, just as Mugabe and Nkomo do.'

Any lingering doubts that I had about the wisdom of the cabinet offer disappeared with Mandela's unfortunate but revealing analogy: after crushing – with considerable violence in Matabeleland – his political opponent and former ally, Joshua Nkomo, Zimbabwean president Robert Mugabe had then co-opted him into government as vice president. This effectively destroyed any prospect of multiparty democracy taking root there. And when, many years later, in 2000, Morgan Tsvangirai and his Movement for Democratic Change (MDC) set about trying to resurrect it, the country was already on the scree-slope towards one-party dictatorship.

The DP's Federal Council accepted my advice that it would be impossible, on the basis outlined by Mandela, for the party to participate in government and simultaneously maintain any role as an opposition. I had also gained the impression – although he never said so – that Mandela was relieved when I indicated that I thought the DP would find it difficult to accept the proposal. It may well have been that significant elements in his own circle jibbed at the idea of one Tony Leon becoming a cabinet minister.

I thanked the president for his 'generosity of spirit and his nation-building efforts of which this move was evidence'. *Die Burger* praised our decision for 'striking a blow for democracy'.[8]

However, writing in the *Pretoria News,* the normally cautious commentator and veteran radio journalist Chris Gibbons let rip at us: 'The decision [by the DP] to remain in opposition will see the party permanently sidelined, with support slowly ebbing away until it vanishes into a richly deserved obscurity.'[9]

Fortunately, events were to prove his prediction almost entirely wrong, and the party in the next decade would increase its support more than eightfold at the national level and enter government in one province and in dozens of local municipalities.

But, in the intervening seventeen years since the temptation of Mandela, I have sometimes grappled with the counter-factuals of the situation, or history's 'what if?' questions. Although I did not enter politics with a view to enjoying the accoutrements of power, exercising executive office would certainly have been an opportunity to put principles and ideas into practice from the very heart of government. But, whatever fleeting thoughts on this I have entertained since declining Mandela's offer, there is a larger truth that Mandela's proposal, and the terms for its acceptance, revealed. South Africa, today, would be less likely to have been a robust, open democracy with government held to account by an independent opposition, had his proposal been realised.

And that, perhaps, from today's vantage point – and with an ANC government *sans* Mandela and stripped of any of his spirit of inclusivity – is the greatest ex post facto justification for that rejection of so many years ago.

CHAPTER TWELVE

Golden Moments

E ARLY ONE SPRING morning in late September 1995, the stillness of an ocean-facing apartment in Clifton, one of the most sought-after enclaves on Cape Town's Atlantic seaboard, was abruptly disturbed by the ringing of a bedside telephone. The apartment belonged to veteran parliamentarian Colin Eglin and his wife, Joyce, who happened to be alone at home at the time. She was startled enough by the call at that hour, but more so when she picked up the receiver.

'Good morning, Mrs Eglin,' the caller said. 'It's Mandela here – is Colin home?'

In her retelling of the telephone tale, Joyce (who sadly died some two years later, in August 1997) didn't believe him, certain that it must be a practical joke. Only once Mandela had managed to convince her, drawing on his considerable powers of persuasion, did she inform him that her husband was overseas.

'Well,' the president said cheerily, 'I just wanted to wish you both a very happy Rosh Hashanah,' his call coinciding with the Jewish New Year festivities then in progress.

After a brief, perhaps slightly embarrassed, pause, Joyce was obliged to disabuse him: 'Actually, Mr President, Colin and I are both Methodists.'

Now there was some perplexed hesitation at the president's end. 'Oh,' Mandela confessed, 'but I thought, with all those years as member of parliament for Sea Point, that Colin and you were Jewish.' Indeed, the constituency Colin had represented since 1974 was significantly Jewish in its demographic make-up; hence Mandela's mistaken assumption.

Joyce recovered quickly enough, however, and suggested to Mandela: 'Perhaps you should call our party leader, Tony Leon. He is actually Jewish, you know.'

'Don't worry,' Mandela informed her with no-doubt-renewed confidence, 'he's next on my list.'

Moments later – and 1400 kilometres away in Orange Grove, Johannesburg – I indeed received Mandela's warm wishes for the New Year. And, doubtless, thereafter he rang many other surprised and delighted denizens of South Africa's Jewish community.

This by no means isolated vignette captures the essence of Mandela's generous spirit of inclusivity; his ability to reach across the divisions of language, race, religion, politics and culture to make the 'Rainbow Nation' a reality (a term coined by Archbishop Desmond Tutu). In a general, rather than religious, sense, he was an ecumenical first citizen.

Many years later, I heard an account of how Mandela's predecessor and, later, deputy president, FW de Klerk parried the curved-ball question thrown at him as to which of the two had been the better president. With a combination of dexterity and diplomacy, De Klerk responded: 'In terms of administration I was the better president, but as the leader of a nation he was the better one.'

Indeed, Mandela, rather like Ronald Reagan across the Atlantic and some years earlier, had a brilliant ability to paint the broad canvas on which he wanted his administration to be portrayed and remembered by posterity, and he certainly omitted no colours or shades from his palette. Like Reagan and, except where some intense personal or political interest was involved, Mandela did not busy himself in too much detail, and ran a presidency of both famous intimacy and some detachment from the daily happenings in governance.

There was also a degree of shrewd political calculation behind his grand gestures. By embracing all South Africans, he protected the government against any claims that the fine print of legislation, then being steamrollered through parliament and his party conferences, contradicted or undermined the non-racial terms of settlement explicitly embodied in the new constitution and its first president. But each act, doubtless for the impatient race warriors in his midst and alongside him in government, also diminished some of his vast reserves of political capital within his own movement. Some of the larger contradictions between presidential gesture and policy reality will be considered in the next chapter.

Far below Mandela, in the restive platoons of the ANC rank and file, there were occasional glimpses of how illusory some party members thought the Rainbow Nation presidency to be. For example, in November 1997, new meaning was given to the adage *in vino veritas* when an ANC Cape Town metropolitan councillor, Mzukizi Gaba, was caught driving dangerously, and severely inebriated, by two traffic officers. He reportedly turned belligerently on his (presumably pale) interdictors to warn: 'When Mandela dies we will kill you whites like flies.'

Gaba was convicted of drunken driving and given a hefty fine and suspended jail sentence – but his fly-swatting threat still pops up in justification for the call to arms of the so-called South Africa Project (one among an array of incubators of Internet racism), which, from the safety of Louisiana, USA, urges its readers to 'Wake Up or Die White Man'.[1] Far more sober and influential party members than Councillor Gaba would, even on Mandela's watch and with accelerated purpose thereafter, move to reset the political and racial terms of trade in the country.

But Mandela realised the potency of using symbolic healing to bind the wounds of his deeply divided nation. He used his power of patronage to reward old enemies, such as former hardline prison commissioner Jannie Roux, with an ambassadorship.

An even scarcer resource, presidential face time, was also spent on former enemies and their families. He arranged a luncheon at his Pretoria residence for the widows of the iron-fisted National Party era, of Hans Strijdom and John Vorster, and the wife of PW Botha, whom he paired with the surviving spouses of struggle heroes Steve Biko and Moses Kotane, thoughtfully noting: 'These are the wives of the heroes of both sides ... we have fought our fights in the past. We have forgotten it now. We must build a new South Africa.'[2]

Since she was too frail to attend this luncheon, Mandela then flew to the whites-only enclave of Orania for a tea party with Betsie, the widow of assassinated prime minister and apartheid architect Dr HF Verwoerd.

He hosted a lunch for his pitiless prosecutor in the Rivonia Trial,

Dr Percy Yutar. His great light and personal warmth was in evidence everywhere.

Beyond calculation, his authorised biographer Anthony Sampson suggested, these moments indicated that 'his reconciliation was also part of the basic optimism which Mandela had carried with him since his youth, and which was strengthened rather than weakened in jail'. But the author also quoted one of Mandela's colleagues as saying, '"You never quite know … whether he's a saint or a Machiavelli".'[3] Probably a bit of both informed his signature nation-building moments, would have been my conclusion.

In November 2013, some months before South Africans headed to the polls for their fifth democratic general elections, Cyril Ramaphosa, the man so many believed to be the avatar of non-racial constitutionalism, struck a discordant note. He was now ANC deputy president, after a decade in self-imposed political exile. During this time he accrued billions in business while sitting out the presidency of arch political rival Thabo Mbeki. His political star under Mbeki's successor, Jacob Zuma, had risen even as his presumed spirit of inclusivity lessened. During a voter registration drive, he told an audience in his home province of Limpopo, 'If you don't vote, the Boers will come back to control us.' Responding to the outcry from opposition and media quarters, he later 'clarified' his meaning, explaining that he meant it as a reference to 'former apartheid oppressors', not whites or Afrikaners as a group.[4]

But it is noteworthy how Mandela's presidency – nearly two decades before Ramaphosa's dire warning – was marked by his close attention to assuaging the concerns of the recently dethroned white Afrikaner political elite and their followers.

Apart from leaving most of the old order generals of the security establishment in their police and military posts – initially at least, and with ANC understudies who were intended to replace them – Mandela also lavished great attention and care on my parliamentary neighbour, General Constand Viljoen, leader of the right-wing Freedom Front.

Viljoen, white-haired and with piercing blue eyes, cut a physically compact figure. In stark contrast to my own undistinguished and compulsory career, post-school, as a conscript in the army, Viljoen had been described both by admiring colleagues and by subordinates as 'a soldier's soldier'; he rose to the very top of the military machine under President PW Botha, ultimately serving as Chief of the SA Defence Force. During South Africa's military incursion into Angola at the height of the first phase of its civil war in 1975–1976, Viljoen's hands-on military leadership – parachuting into battle with his troops during Operation Savannah – won him widespread admiration across all ranks.

After Viljoen retired from military service in 1985, his farming ventures were constantly interrupted by calls on him to lead a right-wing resistance to the reformist agenda being pursued by government. During the negotiations process inaugurated by De Klerk, the pressure on Viljoen intensified. He was a far more credible leader for the forces of Afrikaner reaction than the brutal but buffoonish AWB leader Eugene Terre'Blanche or the dour parliamentary leadership of the Conservative Party, and posed a much more serious danger to the incipient and fragile democratic order than any other figure on the rejectionist landscape. In the tumultuous final year of negotiations in 1993, he had, together with other white rightists and black homeland holdouts, including Buthelezi, joined in the 'Freedom Alliance'.

But his brief leadership of paramilitaries in the failed Bophuthatswana invasion convinced him that, to adapt Churchill's phrase, 'jaw jaw is better than war war'. Or, as he, more earthily and colloquially, described his last-minute decision to lead a political formation in the 1994 elections, the Freedom Front: '*As hulle kan veg vir Suid-Afrika, kan hulle stem vir Suid-Afrika*' (If they can fight for South Africa, they can vote for South Africa).

Viljoen's iconic status on the white right in fact saw his new movement nose ahead of the Democratic Party in the election and he led a party of nine MPs. We were seated next to each other on the parliamentary frontbenches reserved for leaders of smaller parties. We also shared accommodation on the fifth floor of the parliamentary building reserved for the opposition.

In the ensuing seven years, until he quit politics in 2001, I got to know Viljoen and his delightful and devoted wife, Risti, quite well. He was charming and humorous and, like Mandela, very secure in his own skin. He too was constantly singled out by the president for compliments and chats; perhaps more than many other figures then in politics, he had lessened the thunder of violent reaction by the disaffected right. Viljoen, quite one of the most genuine and unlikely figures I ever encountered in the world of politics, was sincere when he spoke of 'the great mutual trust and regard' between Mandela and himself.[5]

I was never much troubled by the, on occasion, bare-knuckled response some of my and the party's critique of ANC governance received from Mandela in comparison to his relatively benign responses to the Freedom Front's often more robust assessments of government missteps. But the difference in treatment did concern some in my ranks. During a visit to Mandela's home on one occasion, I was accompanied by close friend and senior party official Cecil Bass, who remained silent during my fairly lengthy interaction with the president until, towards the end of our discussion, he asked Mandela, 'Why are you so soft on Viljoen and yet sometimes so critical of the Democratic Party?'

Mandela responded, 'I believe that Viljoen saved South Africa from a civil war by his last-minute agreement to participate in the 1994 elections. I am extremely grateful to him and that is why I am so gentle in my responses to him.'

Yet, as he so often made clear in our discussions, Viljoen drew a sharp distinction between his admiration for Mandela and his fundamental disagreement with the ANC. As a political tactician, he was not as astute as he had been as a battlefield commander; while he earned a very respectful hearing from the normally restive ANC ranks in parliament, not a single suggestion he made in debate was ever acted upon.

Hundreds of stories from enthralled, and mostly ordinary, South Africans, across the normal divides of the country's polity, attested to (and were breathlessly reported by an admiring and largely uncritical media) the potency of the 'Madiba magic'. This became the catch-all moniker for Mandela's sure-footed, feel-good touch that seemed to embrace the entire nation. He proudly boasted to me one Sunday, during a visit to his Houghton home, that he had been 'out and about' recruiting members for the ANC for the forthcoming local government election. 'And', he proclaimed, 'I signed up 127 of them this morning!'

Given that the area had been my political constituency for some years and was regarded as an opposition stronghold, I found this disclosure somewhat discomforting, as Mandela doubtless intended it to be. All I could think of to counter him with was the rejoinder, 'Well, who can say "No" to you, Mr President? But, on election day, they will still vote for us!' Happily, the large majority achieved by the DP candidate against Mandela's man a few weeks later confirmed my prediction.

But it was on 24 June 1995, in the high citadel of South African rugby, the Ellis Park Stadium in Johannesburg, that I witnessed for myself, from a capacity-packed stand far above the field, the moment when Nelson Mandela irrevocably won the heart of white South Africa. By appearing on the field in a Springbok cap and the national squad's green-and-gold jersey, bearing the captain's number 6, Mandela not only earned a roaring ovation from the overwhelmingly white crowd, but also almost certainly helped edge the team to an against-the-odds victory, achieved with a heart-stopping drop goal in extra time, against the more fancied New Zealand All Blacks. South Africa had won its first-ever Rugby World Cup, and Mandela had grafted the most cherished symbol of white, and especially Afrikaner, sporting passion on to his equally cherished nation-building project with quite spectacular results.

There was of course an even more powerful and dramatic back story to the glittering and gritty final that day, and Mandela's role as the team's unofficial 16th man. Appropriately, since he was certainly one of the most gifted and courageous journalists to have covered South Africa's transition from apartheid to democracy, John Carlin – who later became a good family friend of ours – decided to write a book about that World Cup epiphany, *Playing the Enemy*, which was made into the movie *Invictus*, directed by Clint Eastwood, some years later.

When the film was premiered in 2009/2010, I had recently been appointed as South African ambassador to Argentina – the only country in the entire Americas where rugby, played at an internationally competitive level, has a mass following. We thus arranged for one of the Springbok heroes of the 1995 squad, Joost van der Westhuizen, the winning scrum half, to do the honours at the embassy's movie night. Interestingly, he assured the audience that '90 per cent of what you see in the film and the huge role which Mandela played behind the scenes actually happened'.

There is one piece of dialogue in the movie – whether sexed up by a Hollywood scriptwriter or based on original sources is unknown – which, perhaps better than most other presidential encounters memorialised on celluloid, distilled the essence of Mandela's self-appointed task as builder of a new nation, and why he was uniquely equipped for the role. Mandela, played on screen by Morgan Freeman (a very impressive cinematic *Doppelgänger*), is seen engaging with the national sports committee, which is keen on dumping both the Springbok name and emblem, precisely because both were so cherished by those the ANC-aligned committee saw as the white overlords of the apartheid era. Mandela/Freeman rejects the decision, noting, 'That is selfish thinking; it does not serve the nation.' Then, facing the camera, and presumably speaking to South Africa's whites, for whom the Springboks have an almost religious significance, he says, 'We have to surprise them with our restraint and generosity.'

This 'restraint and generosity' would be much required in the period immediately following the rugby triumph, as the country's Truth and Reconciliation Commission (TRC) – headed by the only other South African who approximated Mandela's moral stature, Archbishop Desmond Tutu – exposed both in detail and with some selectivity, the horrors of the country's human rights transgressions.

Established by the Promotion of National Unity and Reconciliation Act of 1995, the TRC was set up to obtain and ventilate testimony from victims and gather information about human rights violations between 1 March 1966 and 5 December 1993; consider applications for amnesty from prosecution for perpetrators; and recommend a system of reparations for victims.

In sum, the TRC investigated 31 000 cases in three years, presenting President Mandela with an interim report in October 1998 of over a million words. Almost from the outset, the composition of the Commission (weighted strongly in favour of the ANC), its terms of reference, and its *modus operandi* were hugely contested.

The TRC – and reactions to it – cast most of the major political players in a poor light.[6] Thabo Mbeki argued that different standards of justice had to be applied to the ANC and the apartheid government: one side had been morally right, the other morally wrong. He was backed by certain in-house intellectuals, who wanted the TRC to go further in blaming and punishing whites in general. Mbeki was also supported by the ANC's ideological prejudices – its 'penchant for self-exoneration' in Martin Meredith's words.[7]

When the final report came out, the ANC was not satisfied that the TRC had read history in its favour; it wanted references to its sins expunged. These related to events ranging from torture to executions in its camps in exile, and to damning conclusions regarding the reign of terror conducted by Mandela's then wife, Winnie Madikizela-Mandela.

Mbeki even sought, via a court challenge, to stop publication of the TRC's interim report. He failed. In response, Tutu threatened to resign: 'If parties are able to grant themselves amnesty,' he fumed, 'what is the point of having a Truth Commission?'[8] More alarming was the ANC's attempt to use its political leverage to force the TRC to rewrite its final report. Mbeki continued to maintain that the TRC had been 'wrong and misguided', despite Mandela's endorsement of its findings.[9] Mandela's role here, in stark contrast to his successor Mbeki's, proved in my view how at crucial moments he could ascend from partisan combatant to leader of the nation.

Whatever unhappiness the leadership of the ANC and Inkatha Freedom Party (IFP) displayed towards the TRC, they both ran a very distant second to the harsh gaze of the commission's focus on De Klerk and the NP. In part, this was – as De Klerk was later to complain bitterly – due to the bias in the TRC and to serious lapses in its procedural conduct and evaluation of evidence. But, overwhelmingly, the weight of information and the nature and conduct of the apartheid government placed the burden of opprobrium on De Klerk's head, as the extant NP leader and as a serving cabinet minister during the apotheosis of apartheid.

The NP's security state was put on public display – from the grotesque and ghoulish detail of its killing machine, presided over by the head of the Vlakplaas special defence unit, Dirk Coetzee, to aspects of chemical warfare, right through to the murder of Steve Biko and the Cradock Four. TRC vice chairperson, Alex Boraine, described the revelations with some feeling as 'a huge sewer spilling out its filth and stench'.[10] It was all broadcast live on radio and TV, daily, and probably did more than anything else to undermine the claims of the NP to a permanent and rejuvenated place in the new South Africa. Former president PW Botha, on whose watch most of the abuses and violations occurred, simply refused to obey a subpoena calling him to testify.

De Klerk, however, appeared three times. Many in his circle told me the TRC was nothing more than a witch-hunt. A prominent Afrikaans-speaking editor said it was directed at railroading the Afrikaner minority as a whole (and not simply its political leadership) into a position of 'permanent moral inferiority'.

At De Klerk's second appearance at the TRC on 14 May 1997, he apologised for all the hardship and suffering caused by apartheid,[11] but reaffirmed his assertion that murder and torture never formed part of government policy – although he was careful to qualify this by referencing it to his period at the helm from 1989 onward.

The TRC did not exhaustively complete its investigations into the abuses of the apartheid regime, and even less so of the conduct of the forces of liberation. This left victims feeling unfulfilled, and suspicions hanging in the air.

It was, however, a few months before Tutu presented Mandela with his TRC report that the person who would become closest to me in matters of the heart was to experience the Mandela touch first-hand.

Mandela had always maintained a lively interest in my romantic attachments, and had often urged me, aged thirty-seven at the start of his presidency, to change my single status and get married. At the time of the July 1998 state visit to South Africa of the mercurial president of Ghana, Flight Lieutenant Jerry Rawlings, I was involved in a serious relationship with a bright and beautiful Israeli divorcée, Michal Even-Zahav, who accompanied me to the state banquet Mandela hosted for the Ghanaian at the Presidential Guest House in Pretoria.

It was Michal's first experience of attending such an event, and it was memorable in at least two respects. First, Rawlings made a speech of such rambling incoherence and length that I, along with other bemused guests, assumed he was, in the idiom, 'high' on some substance or other.

Michal's dinner experience was memorable for another reason, too. When the protracted formalities were winding down, I received the usual summons from a presidential aide to present myself at the top table – but this time I was advised to bring 'my partner' with me. Mandela grasped both of Michal's hands and asked: 'When are you going to say "Yes" to this young man?' Michal blushed and gave a non-committal response; not for the first time, the president had pre-empted me.

Some two and a half years later, on 10 December 2000, Michal and I were married in Cape Town, and Mandela was among the first to congratulate us when we met the day after the wedding.

CHAPTER THIRTEEN

Tolerant to a Fault

ICHAL'S ENCOUNTER with Mandela at the state banquet for
the Ghanaian president proved at one undemanding level how I
accommodated myself and the party to aspects of Mandela's embrace of,
and invitations to, the world at large. I also quite enjoyed my encounters,
which ranged from substantive meetings to just five minutes of chitchat,
with some of the more powerful and interesting figures on the global
stage who wished to bathe in the light of his presidency.

However, I drew some red lines back then to this hobnobbing with
the world's political elite – I declined the offer of a meeting with Iranian
president Hashemi Rafsanjani in August 1996, and, when Fidel Castro
received a hero's welcome in parliament in October 1998, the DP benches
were empty, following our caucus decision to boycott the event.

This drew howls of outrage from the ANC, the media and the occasionally crude but exquisitely politically apt cartoonist Zapiro (Jonathan

Shapiro), who penned my caricature with the caption: 'I have a double standard to maintain.'

The government's posturing overtures to rogue regimes and dictators were one thing – I thought them counterproductive to the national interest, though perhaps in the overall schema they were marginal and even harmless.

But it did reveal a disconnect, indeed a gaping contradiction, between stated principle on the eve of assuming power, and conduct in office afterwards. I had, perhaps naively, taken at face value the most famous expression of the pivot of our international relations under the new order, penned by Mandela himself in late 1993, just months before his election as president. Writing in the influential journal *Foreign Affairs* on the topic 'South Africa's Future Foreign Policy', he proclaimed unambiguously: 'South Africa's future foreign policy will be based on our belief that human rights should be the core concern of international relations ...'[1]

Invocations of principle before shouldering the testing burden of power yielded to other imperatives after its assumption. But, to be strictly fair, Mandela had left several clues about the difference between intention and result even before he was inaugurated. Most of this related to the funding needs of his party, which guzzled cash faster than it could be raised.

I was first made aware of this when I visited Taiwan as a guest of its government at the end of 1994. Our ambassador there (we still maintained diplomatic links) cheerfully told me that when, before the election, Mandela visited the pariah island, as mainland China designated it, he directly requested the staggering amount of US $10 million from President Lee Teng-hui. The full amount was granted 'within minutes'.

But, although Mandela was absolutely candid when pressed on this issue by the media a year later, he claimed 'the money was given as "a donation and not a bribe"'.[2]

Taiwan's largesse to the ANC – buttressed by a further R14 million donation in 1995 for a Defence Force vocational training scheme – did not prevent South Africa from severing diplomatic ties with the island state in November 1996, in line with the worldwide trend of recognising only one China, namely Beijing.

In the case of Taiwan, which by the time of Mandela's visit had adopted democracy, it could at least be squared with his nostrum on human rights. But in this taxonomy it was an outlier, and the ANC spread its funding net very wide indeed. Suharto of Indonesia – whose uninterrupted thirty-two-year dictatorship was, with a welter of supporting evidence, described by the *New York Times* as 'one of the most brutal and corrupt of the twentieth century'[3] – became an apparently enthusiastic and significant cash donor to Mandela's party coffers. In 1995, for example, Mandela thanked the incoming Indonesian ambassador for Suharto's '"generous financial assistance" to his party',[4] and, in November 1997, he personally conferred on the Indonesian leader the highest state honour, the Order of Good Hope.

The contradiction that existed between bestowing this gong and the Indonesian's ruthless suppression of the independence movement of East Timor, which the ANC supported, and the dictator's fierce anti-Communism, which the party detested, was never explained. But, whatever inconsistency his fraternising with the dubious Suharto revealed, it did at least leave a more durable mark: one of Mandela's biographers, Tom Lodge, noted that it was the Indonesian who first presented

Mandela – doubtless along with the cash – with his comfortable and colourful 'tunic-like shirts', which became 'the distinctive attribute of the "Madiba" sartorial style'.[5]

The truth was that no one could raise funds for the ANC quite like Mandela. He told me that in his first year out of prison he raised a staggering R66 million for his party from African leaders alone. As in Asia, so nearer to home, Mandela was not at all ideological, requesting and receiving funds from such mutual enemies as Angola's José Eduardo dos Santos and Zaire's Mobutu Sese Seko. The ANC's attachment to the Polisario Front did not preclude Mandela from seeking and receiving cash from its nemesis, the king of Morocco. He succeeded with every African potentate he called on – bar, he advised, Egypt's Hosni Mubarak.

Party-political fundraising in South Africa remains a wild and unregulated frontier, without limits or prohibitions. After the ANC assumed power, I received credible reports of how official state visits were used, in part, to canvass these funds. When the DP attempted to probe this point we were met with non-answers, not denials.[6]

What influence such financial grubbing had on foreign policy posturing was difficult to discern. When challenged about his close links with Libyan strongman Muammar Gaddafi – at the time a fomenter of terrorism abroad and repression at home – Mandela simply advised the enquiring reporter to 'go jump in the pool',[7] as he quaintly expressed it then. I continued to question the Libyan link, which led to that country's energetic ambassador to South Africa asking to meet me. We did so in my Johannesburg home and his easy charm was as disarming as his 'gift of friendship to the DP', a bottle of Chivas Regal – surprising, I thought, given its Muslim provenance.

But the Libyan connection was as consistent – it was to extend under President Zuma even beyond the point at which Gaddafi was besieged in his own country shortly before his execution by rebel forces there in 2011 – as it was disturbing.

In this regard, I much enjoyed a parliamentary tea session that visiting US President Bill Clinton, democratic in all senses of the word, hosted for the parliamentary opposition during his state visit to South Africa in March 1998. His legendary intelligent charm and charisma were on full display that afternoon. But far more revealing and disconcerting than my altogether memorable personal encounter with the US president on that day was an account of an incident during the same visit, which I received many years later from a senior US government official.

It revealed how Mandela had ambushed his distinguished American visitor on behalf of his Libyan friend, and, at the time, international pariah, Gaddafi. Usually, every encounter on a tightly choreographed state visit is agreed by officials in advance. But, during a private meeting between the two heads of state in Mandela's Tuynhuys office, Mandela theatrically, and apparently much to Clinton's displeasure, announced that a third person would be joining the meeting. At this point, there entered the immensely influential Saudi ambassador to the US, Prince Bandar, to negotiate American acceptance of Mandela's proposal of trying the Libyan suspects of the Pan Am Lockerbie aircraft bombing at a neutral venue, rather than their being extradited to the US or to Scotland. Despite the fury of the officials accompanying Clinton, this extremely unorthodox diplomacy ultimately led to precisely this result: in 2000, under Scottish law, the bombers were tried, then convicted, in a special court in the Netherlands.

On another famous occasion, at a Commonwealth summit in November 1995, Mandela broke ranks with fellow African leaders, who traditionally practised in public the 'three monkeys' injunction to hear no evil, see no evil and speak no evil in respect of even their most tyrannical peers. Mandela was infuriated by the decision of the Nigerian dictator Sani Abacha to order the execution of human rights activist Ken Saro-Wiwa during the conference, and immediately called for Nigeria's suspension from the Commonwealth and for sanctions to be imposed against its regime. There were few takers for this hardline approach, however – either at the summit, or even among his foreign affairs team back home. He had, in the words of one observer, '[e]xperienced the limits of moral authority as a diplomatic weapon'.[8]

The hard fact was that South Africa's foreign policy under the aegis of Mandela, and more so under his successor, Mbeki, was contested terrain. It was never clear or consistent. The designated minister, Alfred Nzo, was amiable but ineffective and inert, and policy lurched between high-minded principle and lowest-common-denominator, Third World struggle solidarity.

While the ANC leadership greatly enjoyed hobnobbing with the G-7 (as it then was), it appeared equally happy rubbing the West the wrong way by parading its allegiance with the countries and regimes that lost the Cold War.

CHAPTER FOURTEEN

Cash Complex

Back at home, similar impulses were evident both in fashioning and in effecting domestic policy. Some of this was due to the meagre fiscal inheritance Mandela was bequeathed. There was a sharp contradiction between the ambitions of the ANC in opposition – for example, to build a million new houses in five years, and other large promises embedded in its Reconstruction and Development Programme (RDP) – and the unwelcome realities they had to confront on assuming office.

Martin Meredith provided a useful, if sombre, snapshot:

> Mandela discovered ... that South Africa's economy was in dire straits. The ANC had expected to inherit an economic cornucopia; its ambitious development plans were based on that notion. But the coffers, in fact, were nearly empty. The previous government had run up a record budget deficit of 8.6 per cent of gross domestic product, and

gross foreign exchange reserves had fallen to less than the equivalent of three weeks of imports ... The cost of debt service together with current expenditure consumed 92 per cent of government revenue, leaving only 8 per cent for capital spending.[1]

Mandela and his close lieutenants understood soon enough what this meant. His transport minister, Mac Maharaj, explained the limits of the new reality: "'There was simply no money to do what we had planned ... We had to dump our blueprints and start from the beginning.'"[2] Mandela outsourced most of the decision-making and detail of economic policy to his kitchen cabinet of party insiders – particularly party heavyweights Max Sisulu and Ketso Gordhan and ministers Tito Mboweni (who headed labour), trade and industry's Trevor Manuel, and Deputy Finance Minister Alec Erwin, and, most notably, Deputy President Thabo Mbeki. But he also drew in outsiders, to restore the restive and unpredictable markets. His first two ministers of finance – Derek Keys and Chris Liebenberg – were drawn from the world of white business and banking, and at the Reserve Bank he retained the monetary hawk Dr Chris Stals, who, like Keys, had been appointed to office by the previous NP government. It was only after the ANC found its feet in government, after 1996, that it moved Manuel into the finance hot seat; three years later, it sent Mboweni to the Reserve Bank.

The difficulty confronting Mandela's government in navigating the straits between fiscal limits and the soaring expectation of its mass of supporters, along with the powerful interests of its alliance partners in the trade unions, became quickly apparent.

Mandela made a significant contribution to resolving this conundrum.

By his own estimation, he understood little of either economic theory or practice, but grasped one big thing better than the romantic socialists and other hard men and women of the left in his ideologically capacious organisation: he knew that only rapid economic growth and large infusions of investment, especially from abroad, could help South Africa create the jobs for the burgeoning ranks of the unemployed, and provide the revenue stream, via taxation, to fund the services government had promised. He had also undergone his own Damascene conversion in the rarefied atmosphere of Davos back in 1992, well out of earshot of the siren calls of nationalisation.

Few local or overseas business people were immune to the Mandela charm, and he personalised his relationships with them to good effect, especially when raising funds for specific projects, and his ever-better-endowed Children's Fund. There was also a darker undertow to this fraternisation with many in the business elite, who were seen by some in his movement as both race and class enemies.

On the day of Mandela's death on 5 December 2013, one of the most acute and generally admiring obituaries of him penned by veteran journalist David Beresford was published in *The Guardian*. He recorded, post-mortem, what had been much spoken of, in elite circles at least, when Mandela was alive, about his 'attachment to the glamour of the very rich'. Beresford continued:

> For the boy in ragged trousers, who had to struggle right up to the time [Rivonia Trial judge Quartus] De Wet removed him from the world of financial responsibility, money was dazzling. Hence, once freed, he holidayed at the Irish businessman Sir Tony O'Reilly's

Caribbean island and gave the go-ahead for his takeover of South Africa's biggest newspaper group ... He allowed the casino king, Sol Kerzner, to host the wedding of his daughter Zinzi. He borrowed rich men's houses and flew around South Africa in their aircraft. In speeches, he often used to boast of his ability to milk wealthy businessmen for good causes. But, at times, there was suspicion as to how 'good' – or, more specifically, how independent of his own interests – these good causes were.[3]

For example, Beresford cited how Mandela indulged various fundraising schemes that bordered on the tawdry, including 'his emergence in 2003 as a talented painter', dashing off sketches of Robben Island apparently with 'a little help' from an artist who was, by bizarre circumstance, the granddaughter of PW Botha. Then there was his approach to a group of wealthy businessmen for donations to support him and his family via a trust, which apparently in five years (2003–2008) received R18,5 million. His obituarist noted tartly, 'There does not appear to be a charitable dimension to this fund outside the Mandela family.'[4]

This particularly warring, often unattractive, family were already squabbling over Mandela's estate before he was dead.

One emissary, despatched by a multinational corporation to Mandela to meet him and hand over a donation, told me in later years how the great man had looked at him 'rather coldly' and returned the proffered cheque for R500 000, advising that he expected 'double the amount'. Apparently the company, suitably chastened, later complied.

After his retirement, I met Mandela at his impressive private Cape Town residence in the leafy, ultra-expensive suburb of Bishopscourt. He told me he had bought the house from the former boss of insurance giant Old Mutual, Mike Levett. 'And I bargained him right down on its price,' Mandela boasted laughingly. He also advised that after his purchase he had obtained from Old Mutual a donation to build a school in an amount near the cost of the home!

In some matters of policy Mandela was unyielding to the entreaties of big business. For example, shortly before parliament agreed the final constitution in early May 1996, organised business was pressing for the entrenchment in the constitution of the right to lock out striking workers during an industrial dispute, along with the right to strike, which had already been agreed. Cosatu embarked on a national strike, illegal as it happened, to express its opposition to this demand. I had been beseeched via fax by Leslie Boyd, deputy chairman of Anglo American and a supporter of my party, to 'declare a dispute in the negotiations', given the lopsided direction in which the labour relations clause in the constitution was headed. I therefore requested a meeting with Mandela, and we duly met at his Houghton home on the evening of Sunday 28 April – just days before parliament was set to vote on the constitution.

Boyd had not been alone in his concern. A business delegation opposed to the constitution's tilt to the demands of trade unions had spent ten hours that very day with Mandela. It appeared that there had been neither concessions nor a meeting of minds at that meeting and, doubtless, Mandela was tired both of the issue and of any further entreaties by the time we met that evening.

He told me, quite bewilderingly, that business as a whole was 'quite satisfied' with the proposal to exclude the right to a lock out from the constitution. I had, however, taken the precaution of bringing Boyd's fax, and invited Mandela to read it. He airily dismissed its contents on the basis that 'Les Boyd is a fire-eater' – a strange response, I thought, to one of the titans of South African industry. I was later informed by Marinus Daling, executive chairman of the financial conglomerate Sanlam, that the talks had proceeded extremely badly. 'What could we do?' he asked me. 'We have to go along to get along'.

In terms of attracting sustained levels of investment in South Africa's stalling economy, however, a consensus across both business and government was emerging that something beyond presidential phone calls and face time was needed. And his deputy, Thabo Mbeki, realised that what was required was a shift in gear. By 1996, after a sharp fall in the value of the currency, the RDP was formally abandoned and its ministry closed down. In its stead came GEAR (Growth, Employment and Redistribution), which promised high growth rates (6 per cent by the year 2000), a million new jobs in exchange for structural economic reforms, including trade liberalisation, and sharp reductions in inflation and the fiscal deficit. Would this lure the investors?

Aside from a run on the rand, GEAR's arrival coincided with and doubtless was triggered by a very nasty turn in the economic winds buffeting the country. On one hand, government programmes soon enough, if unevenly, had started to transform lives, especially of the rural poor, in their provision of sanitation, education and primary health care. But rising crime and slow employment growth, on the back of investor skittishness about emerging markets generally, meant many of the other promised deliverables, from housing to jobs, could not be obtained in an atmosphere of 'declining business confidence'.[5]

As with so many other ambitious programmes, this one was only half implemented. The government did impressive work – in the teeth of stern dissent from its alliance partners – in repairing the country's balance sheet and opening up its economy. The budget deficit and the rate of inflation were sharply reduced.

But, of course, Mandela, though not a red-in-tooth-and-claw socialist by the time he entered the presidency, was no free market evangelist, and both his inclination to conciliation and his hugely diverse support base meant that he had to perform a careful double act. In the opinion of the *Financial Times*, this meant '[h]e strived for a liberal economic policy that balanced the need for radical redistribution of wealth with the demands of economic growth'.[6]

Certainly there was a reversal of capital flight, and, within eighteen months of assuming office, his Reserve Bank governor, Stals, was amazed to report that, beyond expectation, a then-record net amount of R30 billion had flowed into the country from abroad, and both the bond market and local bourse surged with activity, much of it foreign.[7] By the third year of his presidency, in 1997, a quite impressive R12 billion in foreign direct investment, especially compared to the disinvestment that hallmarked the predecessor regime, was recorded.[8] [9]

But the promised jobs did not materialise, largely because the millions sitting at the bottom of the labour market, with scant skills and training, were unable to enter it.

In the face of demands from the trade unions and the left, parliament noddingly approved ever-tighter restrictions on the labour market and abandoned the process of privatisation before it was ever commenced. GEAR's growth targets and job creation promises could only have been met had the policy been implemented coherently and completely.

From my vantage point on parliament's labour committee, and despite my solitary opposition, I watched a quartet of bills (ranging from a wholly new Labour Relations Act to the racially loaded and skills-crushing Employment Equity Act) give the left a chance to claw back from the free market, via the back door, the hostages that Mandela had released through the front. Little wonder then that, by the end of Mandela's presidency in 1999, South Africa's growth rate was just over half the promised figure, at around 3.5 per cent, and, instead of the anticipated boost in employment, we had shed half a million jobs, and unemployment was rising.[10]

CHAPTER FIFTEEN

Lapses of Loyalty

IF THE NEED to reconcile often irreconcilable stakeholders in the South African economy meant the result achieved was the best obtainable at the time, the same cannot be said either for the rapid emergence of a cronyist rent-seeking capitalist class, or for the creeping corruption that infected the newly democratised body politic shortly after Mandela's presidency began.

In this, early examples suggested, Mandela was careless at best, and, in some cases, even complicit, with public office being seen by some as a short cut to personal riches. This trend accelerated under his successors in office, but early warning bells rang loudly during his presidency and he did not do much to answer the alarm. It is certainly true that, in the corruption scandals manifested on his watch, there was not the slightest hint of any self-enrichment by Mandela himself. This was in studied contrast to President Jacob Zuma, who, a decade and a half later, clearly benefited to a staggering extent from state-funded improvements to his rural home at Nkandla in KwaZulu-Natal. But instead of establishing any form of self-denying ordinances for politicians during his pioneering presidency, Mandela did the opposite: he too often indulged the transgressors.

Our small parliamentary opposition party, invigorated by some in the media, was deeply immersed in exposing three of these scandals and in probing the errant officials involved. In each case, however, Mandela backed the wrongdoers and ignored, indeed undermined, his famous commitments to transparency and democratic accountability.

Balefully, the first in this trifecta concerned HIV/AIDS, a scourge that both overwhelmed the country and certainly destroyed much of the credibility of Mandela's successor, Thabo Mbeki. On this life-and-death matter Mandela resolutely refused either to address the causes of the disease or forthrightly to promote its treatment. But he did lend his immense authority to shield his health minister from the consequences of her misuse of targeted funds budgeted for combating the disease, and of lying to parliament in the process.

Dr Nkosazana Dlamini-Zuma, the ex-wife of KwaZulu-Natal party boss and later president, Jacob Zuma, was an imperious member of Mandela's inner circle. She was also 'royal game', it quickly emerged when the scandal broke over the play, *Sarafina II*. She might not have had any coherent strategy for addressing the HIV/AIDS pandemic, but her instincts for the preservation of herself and her ministry were soon clear enough.

Short-circuiting tender procedures, she wasted nearly R14 million on a play produced by her close friend Mbongeni Ngema. It purported to be an 'educational drama' about HIV/AIDS, but soon closed down, and apparently was full of misinformation on the disease. By comparison, the losing bidder in the government tender process offered to produce a similar play for R600 000.[1]

My parliamentary colleague Mike Ellis, who did yeoman service on parliament's health committee, was, initially at least, pleasantly surprised when its chairperson, Dr Manto Tshabalala-Msimang (who would later enter infamy as an AIDS-denying health minister) enthusiastically endorsed his call for the minister to account to the committee, both for her misuse of funds and for her lack of candour in explaining their origins.[2] Tshabalala-Msimang and Dlamini-Zuma were, according to the parliamentary rumour mill, famously at odds.

But, before this committee could conclude its work, Dlamini-Zuma, tearfully apparently, implored Mandela to protect her, and Tshabalala-Msimang was removed from the committee chair – and rewarded with a deputy ministry. Parliament had a surfeit of lawyers, so appointing her to the vacant deputy ministry of justice suggested that something other than the principle of 'fit for purpose' was at play.

Mandela then decided to enter the lists himself, rounding on Dlamini-Zuma's critics, and accusing the 'white-owned media' of victimising her. This led Martin Meredith to the apt conclusion that, in addition to defending the indefensible, he was 'making a racial issue of it for good measure'.[3]

The next scandal was far more serious and more straightforward in terms of both the self-enrichment and the person at its centre. It also concerned another Mandela favourite, the charismatic cleric and ethically challenged ANC Western Cape leader, Dr Allan Boesak.

I was far more directly involved in this matter, since a university friend, a lawyer of ANC inclinations but deep professional probity, Greg Nott, had been commissioned by the Scandinavian agency DanChurch Aid to investigate how Boesak's Foundation for Peace and Justice had diverted over R3 million intended for the poor and destitute. Nott's firm produced a 600-page report, which proved, quite conclusively, that Boesak had enriched himself with the aid agency's proceeds and funded a lavish lifestyle for himself and his wife.

The government, through the office of Deputy President Mbeki, produced a risible and easily rebutted three-page defence of its erring pastor. I dismissed it as an 'effort to whitewash the stain of corruption off Boesak'. To be fair, in this case at least, the cleansing process did not work; Boesak was forced to relinquish the ambassadorship for which he had been earmarked by Mandela. Ultimately he was convicted of theft and corruption, and was sentenced to six years' imprisonment in 1999.

But, once again – at the outset at least – Mandela provided his errant appointee with some cover. He claimed that the government had found charges against 'one of the most gifted young men in the country' to be 'baseless'.[4]

The parliamentary pub, to which I quite often retreated with colleagues after a hard day's sitting, was a useful listening post for cross-party information and gossip. A semi-permanent fixture there during the Mandela presidency was the ANC and SA Communist Party MP, Dr Blade Nzimande. His star, which went into deep descent under Thabo Mbeki, was to shine far brighter when Jacob Zuma became president and he entered the cabinet. But, with Mandela, he had to content himself with a committee chairmanship. He was also quite candid, especially after the second or so glass of his preferred tipple, white wine. One night in August

1996, around the old assembly bar, he lamented that it was 'sickening' how the ANC had been 'corrupted by money', though in good Communist-conspiratorial style, blamed the sickness on the 'capitalist system' rather than on the party. Of course, the headline event that roused Blade to this denunciation had been his party's decision that day to expel from its ranks its popular deputy minister, Bantu Holomisa (who had topped the poll in the elections for the ANC national executive), for testifying against casino king Sol Kerzner and one of the recipients of his largesse, or bribe, Minister for Public Enterprises Stella Sigcau.

This third major stain on the escutcheon of Mandela's government left an unforgiving trace on all players, bar Holomisa, who was cast out of the movement and then founded a party – which soon enough declined both in relevance and in electoral significance.

Ironically, however, when Mandela died in December 2013, it was this political prodigal who emerged as one of the Mandela family insiders, present by invitation at his deathbed. But back then in parliament he earned the wrath of Mandela and the ANC for breaking the local equivalent of the Sicilian code of *omertà,* or silence.

Sigcau, who had impressive lineage as the daughter of the King of the amaPondo in Transkei, and Holomisa had both been props of some stature in the homeland apparatus under apartheid. Sigcau had served as the prime minister of the unrecognised – except by its paymasters in Pretoria – 'Republic of Transkei', and had been deposed in a coup engineered by one of her military generals, none other than Holomisa himself. No doubt there was bad blood between them, but the ANC offered a home to both and they rewarded it with significant votes from the region.

Holomisa's great offence, which the party held to warrant his expulsion, was his appearance before the TRC in August 1996, where he alleged that Kerzner had bribed Sigcau's predecessor, Prime Minister George Matanzima (who, by a further twist of irony, was Mandela's cousin), in whose cabinet she served. Kerzner, it was claimed, paid over R2 million for exclusive gaming rights in the territory. That much had already been in the public domain. But what made Holomisa's charge so incendiary, to the ANC at least, was his disclosure that Sigcau had also received a cut (in the rather measly amount of R50 000) and that Kerzner had paid a further R2 million (obviously his preferred amount for such matters) to the ANC for its 1994 election campaign. I couldn't help smiling to recall how one of my predecessors as party leader, Van Zyl Slabbert, had told me that Kerzner had basically drummed him and his key fundraiser, businessman Tony Bloom, out of his office when he had sought a dona- tion for the liberal Progressive Federal Party, on the basis that the party was 'Communist'.

But no one smiled in the ANC hierarchy when Holomisa added to his testimony this statement: 'As a loyal ANC member I want to resist the inference that the price our organisation had to pay in return for financial assistance was that in the event our organisation became the majority government – as indeed it is now – Sol Kerzner would not be prosecuted.'[5] Kerzner, indeed, was never prosecuted.

Mandela later admitted that Kerzner had 'secretly paid him the money for the ANC election fund', and acknowledged the party had 'seriously mishandled' the matter. But he was unforgiving of what he viewed as Holomisa's 'treachery'.[6]

These events provided almost continuous evidence for my party col- leagues and me in building the case that Mandela's government was 'soft on corruption', which assisted our cause of gaining support among opposition-minded voters. But, in terms of the wider narrative, they also suggest that Mandela was conflicted. There was his sincere respect for the constitution and rule of law, on one hand, and his deep organisational loyalties and ties, on the other. He found it hard to stamp out these practices when they were first manifest.

It was also at more or less the halfway point in his presidency, during 1996–1997, that Mandela's cabinet approved the single most controversial, and almost certainly the most corruption-laden, project of the new government: the Arms Deal. The decision by a special cabinet committee to expend R12 billion (it ultimately amounted to R60 billion) on modernising the South African National Defence Force, in pursuit of 'a strategic defence acquisition' raised the ire of many in civil society, given the myriad social needs and pressing claims on the depleted treasury.

It certainly seemed, to state matters at their mildest, an inversion of priorities for a government that had promised 'a better life for all'. The flagrant contraventions of basic tender procedures, allegations of improper interference in the bidding process and direct meddling in it by Deputy President Thabo Mbeki and especially Defence Minister Joe Modise, and the enrichment of a slew of senior officials, would only surface after Mandela had left office. But this 'original sin' of the new democracy, as the deal came to be characterised, certainly suggested that Mandela was complacent in allowing his defence minister and others to steamroller his preferred bidders through the process, and apparently enrich himself handsomely in exchange.

Modise died before any of the allegations against him could be tested. But, at the very least, Mandela's administration blithely ignored the unenforceability of the 'industrial offsets', which fatuously and inaccurately allowed government to claim that the deal would result in greater financial and economic gains than losses for the treasury and the country. Even at the time of Mandela's death in December 2013, a judicial commission appointed by President Jacob Zuma had barely begun to weigh the evidence that suggested that the deal was contaminated by influence peddling and corruption.

One can look back from today, when a mushroom cloud of corruption engulfs the government, and suggest that, weighed in the balance, these scandals were – in size and extent – almost picayune by comparison. But Mandela had the moral weight and the authority derived from it, never to be equalled, to set an example for his successors – and, by that high standard, he failed.

CHAPTER SIXTEEN

Family Matters

THERE WERE SEVERAL occasions, some already chronicled here and many others published elsewhere, when Mandela's avuncular, and – in the apt description of his authorised biographer[1] – 'dazzling' persona gave way to irritation and even anger. He lashed out, for example, at his close friend Desmond Tutu when the former Anglican Archbishop quipped that the perks-loving, salary-guzzling political class was proof that the country's first democratic government had only 'stopped the gravy train long enough to get on it'.[2] The two got over this quarrel soon enough – but it was obvious that Mandela, despite his invitation to the media and to critics to 'hold up a mirror to the government', did not always enjoy the reflection on display.

In one response he provided early evidence that even a non-racial avatar of his extraordinarily generous disposition, who sustained such disciplined control of his emotions, had clear limits. The mask slipped, in public at least, when, for all the apparent conviction of an oft-repeated mantra about the need for a critical, independent press, he fulminated to editors in November 1996: 'There is a perception among the population that the mass media is controlled by the minority section of the population … [I]t is a totally unacceptable situation in terms of our vision … I seem to feel that the conservative press is trying to preserve, one way or another, the status quo.'[3]

Nor was Mandela at all shy in our many private conversations – or in his public attacks on the opposition from the podium of parliament or at party conferences – about vehemently disputing my and others' criticism of his government's policies or the conduct of his party. I dealt earlier with his near-obsession with 'correcting' and challenging, often in the most intemperate terms, my party's commentary on the ANC cover-up of the Shell House Massacre. The emergence of this 'other Mandela' reached its full and fiery zenith at the ANC Conference in Mafikeng in December 1997.

But there was one subject, far closer to home and nearer to his heart, about which Mandela never once chastised or challenged me, either publicly or privately: my very public opposition to the conduct of his former wife, Winnie Madikizela-Mandela.

In May 1992, before I had first met Mandela – and when he, though estranged from Winnie, was still formally married to her – a fellow MP and I had posed a series of parliamentary questions to Justice Minister Kobie Coetsee about the slapdash, indeed sloppy, and incomplete prosecution of her, and the kidnapping of key witnesses in her high-profile criminal trial. These matters related to the murder of fourteen-year old James Moeketsi Seipei, known more widely to the world by his nickname 'Stompie'.

Despite her claims of innocence and the fabrication of an alibi, which the prosecution made no effort to rebut (and which, post-trial, other witnesses, and, ultimately, the TRC, convincingly demonstrated was false), the court in 1991 had convicted her on four charges of kidnapping and being an accessory to assault. This occurred in the face of the ANC's determination to present the court proceedings as a 'trial of the movement' itself, in the words of its secretary general Alfred Nzo,[4] and the presence in court of Mandela himself and other movement luminaries in support of Winnie. The court was unmoved; the trial judge, calling her 'an unblushing and unprincipled liar' and 'the moving force' behind the kidnappings, sentenced her to four years in jail. Her conviction and sentence were being processed on appeal at the time we raised the matter in parliament.

Both the trial and the events that gave rise to it, a reign of terror that Mrs Mandela had conducted in Soweto in the late 1980s with her so-called Mandela United Football Club, seemed to me, and to some others, to reveal the dark underside of the struggle for freedom in South Africa.

But Winnie, like the movement in which she was such a powerful light, was Janus-faced. In earlier years she had been the beautiful and iconic embodiment of liberation – a profile in courage. Condemned during her husband's long imprisonment to a life of solitary struggle, this young mother of two infant daughters was harassed, banished and imprisoned by the apartheid state. At the time, she epitomised the spirit of defiant and brave resistance. It was precisely this aspect of her that inspired her admirers, a local and international club of leading lights ranging from US Senator Edward Kennedy to my predecessor as MP for Houghton, Helen Suzman.

Such was her spell and the profound admiration she earned that not even Suzman, an apostle of non-violent change, could bring herself to repudiate her friend after her infamously incendiary remark at a funeral in 1986: 'Together, hand in hand, with our boxes of matches and our necklaces we shall liberate this country'. Her endorsement of the grisly necklacing method of murdering 'apartheid collaborators' in the townships – the victim, bound by wire, with a petrol-doused rubber tyre placed round his or her neck, being set alight – brought to the surface the violent methods used by the ANC to force compliance with its *Diktat* across the country.

Although the ANC's internal *Doppelgänger*, the Mass Democratic Movement (MDM),[5] had denounced her, not for the necklacing comment, but after the discovery of Stompie's body in February 1989, the ANC set aside whatever reservations it felt about its *grande dame* when it was unbanned. Seen as a major connector with its more radical base, and the youth in particular, she was installed as head of its social welfare department. Despite appearing alongside her husband after his release, she conducted in public an affair with her deputy in the department, Dali Mpofu. He was decades younger, and had been one of the brighter law students I had lectured at the University of the Witwatersrand, at the very time when his liaison with Mrs Mandela had apparently commenced.

I had no interest in the prurient aspects of her behaviour, except to feel deep sorrow for the public humiliation that she visited on her famous husband. But I had become convinced that Mrs Mandela's extraordinary status at the time of the difficult political transition suggested that she was receiving special treatment from the elite on both sides of the political fence. That her own movement would protect her was perhaps inevitable. But the evasive answers that Justice Minister Kobie

Coetsee provided in parliament and her chronic under-prosecution by his department – for a string of other murders and disappearances, in which she was clearly implicated – convinced me of the official ambivalence to her. Indeed, Coetsee himself, always sphinx-like in his public and private demeanour, had been then President PW Botha's point man when the National Party government first commenced discussions with its most famous prisoner, Nelson Mandela, in the mid-1980s. An observation of seventeenth-century satirist Jonathan Swift – 'Laws are like cobwebs, which may catch small flies but let wasps and hornets break through' – seemed particularly apt and modern in her case.

I thought the demands of simple justice required that Winnie Mandela's many misdemeanours, and her own and the movement's inclination to self-exoneration, should be challenged at every turn. And, for more or less a decade from 1990 onward, I pursued this course.

Perhaps the most notable chronicler of her nefarious activities was journalist John Carlin, then the local bureau chief for *The Independent* of London. His immense and public admiration for Nelson Mandela notwithstanding, Carlin's reports on Mrs Mandela presented in meticulous and gory detail a portrait of a Madame Defarge on steroids, with a Sartre/Fanon-like penchant[6] for gratuitous violence and terror.[7] His accounts revealed that Stompie's murder was merely the visible tip of a blood-soaked iceberg.

Carlin's articles, on which I heavily relied for parliamentary questions and speeches, were noteworthy, not simply for their content, but also for the reaction, or more precisely the non-reaction, to them by Mrs Mandela and her lawyers. Generally, in the face of potentially defamatory and damaging publicity, 'The Lady' (as another British journalist,

Emma Gilbey, dubbed her in an excoriating book on her descent into violence)[8] either sued for defamation or used the threat of legal proceedings to silence or intimidate her critics.

However, Carlin's exposés in all their damning detail drew only silence from Mrs Mandela. In fact, about seven years later, the Truth and Reconciliation Commission (TRC) confirmed the veracity of Carlin's journalism and his chronicle of abuse, torture, kidnapping and murder. The TRC also corroborated my premise about court and police laxity in respect of holding Mrs Mandela to account. In its special investigation into the affairs of the Mandela United Football Club, an organisation that she led, it concluded in 1998:

> The Commission was left with the distinct impression that the attorney-general was at pains not to prosecute her. Madikizela-Mandela's subsequent prosecution in the kidnapping trial [of Stompie] albeit over twenty-seven months after the abductions, suggests that the authorities had been left with no other option in the light of the revelations of [Mandela United Football Club member Jerry] Richardson. *Strategic decisions with regard to the investigation and prosecution of Madikizela-Mandela appear to have been influenced strongly by the political circumstances and sensitivities of this period.*[9] (Author's emphasis)

The TRC also found that Mrs Mandela refused to take responsibility for her wrongdoings, and was 'politically and morally accountable for the gross violations of human rights' committed by her football club. Despite desperate appeals from Tutu, who chaired the Truth Commission, she could not even bring herself to utter an apology to her victims or their families.

The fact that the Appellate Division had in 1992 substituted a 'paltry fine of R15 000' (as I described it in parliament) for her prison sentence in the Stompie matter seemed to prove that not even the highest court in the land, in this case presided over by Chief Justice Michael Corbett, was inured to considerations of political expediency. Extraordinarily, after I had advised parliament that this substituted sentence was 'so lenient as to induce a sense of shock', one of the presiding appeal judges telephoned me in my parliamentary office – never mind the divisions of power he was meant to uphold – to remonstrate with me. But the best that could be said of the court's legal gymnastics was that at least it upheld her conviction, if not the sentence.

Unsurprisingly, the ANC gave Winnie Mandela a top position on its electoral lists in the 1994 election and swept aside any objection, such as my own public statement that, in so doing, it had disregarded its own rule book, which stated plainly that 'common law criminals are barred from seeking public office'.

In justification, and rubbishing the rule of law, the ANC pronounced ex post facto (having never raised this aspect at her trials or afterwards, until the eve of the election) that her conviction for kidnapping would be overlooked as a 'political offence'.

I denounced this piece of fiction as proof that the party had converted itself into 'a new high court', arguing that, demonstrably, Mrs Mandela should not serve in the new parliament. Although many would later emphasise Jacob Zuma's finessing, and damaging, the instruments of judicial process to clear his advance to the presidency, the Winnie saga was perhaps an early sign that the ANC would alter the rule book to suit its ends. Madikizela-Mandela was indeed elected to the new parliament, as was I. Shortly after we were sworn in as MPs she threw her arms around me and burbled, 'We must get to know each other better.' I awkwardly hugged her back.

At that early stage, Winnie Mandela was on an upward trajectory. She was given the benign enough portfolio of deputy minister of Arts, Culture, Science and Technology. Her appointment was justified to me by an ANC heavy who invoked Lyndon Johnson's aphorism: 'It's better to have her on the inside of the tent pissing out, than outside the tent pissing in.'

However, even as she gadded around the world attending film festivals and the like, it did not take long for the old Winnie to re-emerge. In August 1994, she chose a Women's Day debate in parliament to deliver, using parliamentary privilege, a ferocious attack on the 'apartheid courts' and their temerity in daring to judge her by 'white standards'. She scoffed: 'I was found guilty of kidnapping by those apartheid courts which were a disgrace to our judiciary.'[10] The head of the court that convicted her, Chief Justice Corbett, had recently sworn in her husband as president, and had, together with his colleagues, retained his position in post-apartheid South Africa.

She also turned vitriolic attention on me, saying of my querying her fitness for office: 'There are men in this gathering who, in the calm of their Houghtons, literally fiddled and mounted the steps of power while our townships burnt and who today dare to question my membership of this august house.' As for the period of the notorious Mandela United Football Club, she presented herself as the victim: 'I lived in the terror of those times, and was repeatedly burnt by its fires. I did not flinch …

though the press pursued me like a bloodhound.'[11]

In my response to her self-exoneration, I told an audience in Kimberley in the Northern Cape a few days later that her parliamentary performance would enter the annals as 'one of the most stupefying pieces of self-serving hypocrisy yet heard in the Chamber'. I also indicated that it was my intention to raise 'serious questions' in the forthcoming budget debate in parliament on the Department of Justice.

I had prepared intensely for this showdown, having, via John Carlin, been introduced to two family members of Winnie Mandela's victims – Nicodemus Sono and Dudu Chili. Sono, whom I would accompany to the later TRC hearings on the Football Club, had last seen his son, Lolo – bloodied and beaten – in the company of Mrs Mandela in October 1988. He was with her in a Volkswagen combi, and she refused Nicodemus's entreaties for the release of his son, who was never seen alive again. (His body was ultimately found and identified in 2013, though no charges in this matter were ever preferred against Mrs Mandela or anyone else.) On that pitiful day in October 1988, Winnie Mandela merely claimed he was a 'police spy', and drove off with him.

I was well briefed by the family on the matter, as I was in the case of Sibusiso Chili and his cousin Finky Msoni, by senior ANC Women's League member Dudu Chili, Sibusiso's mother and Finky's aunt. Cut to its essence, a court trial in 1989 relating to the murder of Football Club member Maxwell Madondo had led to the State's placing on record that 'the deceased Maxwell Madondo was a member of the football club and *that a decision was made by Mrs Mandela and the Football Club to kill accused No. 1 (Sibusiso Chili) and accused No. 6 (Lerothodi Ikaneng)'*. Unsurprisingly, Chili was given a very light sentence: one year in jail. But Dudu's home had been petrol bombed the day after Madondo was murdered – 'by Winnie's boys and on her orders,' Dudu told me, and her niece, Finky Msoni, died in the blaze. Extraordinarily, Winnie was neither called as a witness by the State, nor charged by it for any of these crimes.

I told parliament in the incendiary justice debate on 26 August 1994 what I had discovered:

> Only this morning I had a conversation with long-time ANC activist Dudu Chili ... she told me of the occasion in February 1989 when a member of the football team known as Dodo came to see her. He told her that Mrs Mandela had just finished chairing a meeting at which it had been decided that Dudu's son, Sibusiso Chili, and Lerothodi Ikaneng should be eliminated. As a consequence of that and an assault on them by the football team one of the members of the football team [Madondo] was murdered.[12]

I got little further in my speech due to the barracking from the government benches – Winnie herself was a conspicuous absentee from the debate – although I did manage to inform parliament of Winnie's role in the disappearance of Lolo Sono; the attempted murder of Lerothodi Ikaneng, and her serious conflict with the Mass Democratic Movement. But the speech was heckled throughout from the unusually (for a Friday afternoon) well-populated ANC benches and, in addition, was interrupted by no fewer than ten points of order, all of them spurious.

These interruptions and my time spent answering them – given I had only a fourteen-minute speaking-turn – meant that I could not quite

finish my speech. I succeeded, nevertheless, in reading my central con-
tention into the record:

> Mrs Mandela chose in her [Women's Day speech earlier that month]
> to address only the question of Stompie Seipei and his murder and
> kidnapping, dismissing her criminal convictions on the self-serving
> basis that she 'was found guilty of kidnapping by those apartheid
> courts which were a disgrace to the judiciary'.[13]

I went on to charge that court records, press reports and interviews suggested a 'string of unsolved crimes, unpunished offenders and a deliber-
ate under-prosecution or laconic police work in all matters with which
Mrs Mandela's name was associated since 1986'.[14]

My speech caused a sensation, and probably generated more media
attention than any I delivered in parliament before or since. It was
the first item on that night's TV news (this was before the ANC had
completed its takeover of the SA Broadcasting Corporation), while the
Weekend Argus led with the headline: 'ANC covers Winnie's tracks as
Leon speaks'. Journalist John MacLennan wrote: 'Members of the ANC
launched a cover-up in parliament of Mrs Winnie Mandela's past by
attempting to shout down DP leader Tony Leon ... Justice Minister
Dullah Omar said he would not dignify the "tirade" with a reply because
Mr Leon was clearly seeking headlines.'

The report continued: 'It is obvious that Mrs Mandela's role is a very
sore point for ANC members who want to reflect an image of clean and
respectable government. Questioned after the debate, one senior source
said: "I just cannot bring myself to talk about her".'[15]

The ANC's laager around Winnie Mandela did not prevent several of its MPs from later approaching me in private, or even via cupped hand in parliament itself, to congratulate me on my 'exposure' of her. Chief among her onside antagonists was Limpho Hani, who sat near me in parliament and was the widow of the more famous Chris. At the time we were on extremely friendly terms. Her dislike of Winnie was naked and she urged me to pursue matters, as indeed I would do over the next few years.[16]

A few days after this parliamentary joust and the ensuing blaze of publicity, my secretary informed me that the 'president wishes to see you'. Oh-oh, I thought to myself, the 'Old Man' must be seething with anger at my put-down of his wife and I'll have to prepare myself for an unpleasant encounter. At the appointed time shortly thereafter, I presented myself at his office in Tuynhuys. He welcomed me – contrary to expectation – most warmly and then said there was a 'sensitive matter' he needed to discuss with me. I braced myself, mental notes at the ready, for a showdown.

Yet, quite extraordinarily, he did not even refer to the Winnie debate, which was still playing itself out in the press. Instead, he needed my 'buy-in' or words to that effect on the travails apparently then afflicting Margot Feist-Honecker, widow of Erich Honecker, the former head of state of the Communist German Democratic Republic (GDR). Mandela explained that her husband, who had died in 1994 in exile in Chile, had left behind a widow who was living in 'direst poverty' in Santiago. I was completely flummoxed when Mandela informed me that 'we must find a way to pay her a pension ... both she and her husband were big supporters of our liberation struggle'.

I wondered why on earth Mandela sought my approval for such a scheme. I pointed out that I could not see how it could be justified for the South African taxpayer to be called on to support a foreign national when, in any event, German social security arrangements were far more generous than our own. I desisted from telling Mandela that, whatever his movement might 'owe' the Honecker family, their repression of their own citizens (I subsequently discovered that the widow Honecker was a leading Communist politician in her own right) hardly created a sympathetic image. Mandela advised me that he was determined to do 'something for her', but nothing further was ever heard on the matter, publicly at least. However, on the more immediate controversy I had so recently caused around his own wife, he uttered not a word.

Perhaps this was because her star was by then moving sharply into the descent: the following year, he stripped her of her deputy ministry for violating protocols relating to an overseas visit, which an ANC insider told me was simply an excuse to get rid of her. Then Mandela divorced her in a blaze of humiliating and excruciating publicity that cast her in the most severe, philandering and money-grubbing light. Her attempts to be nominated for high office from the floor of the ANC's 1997 conference were rebuked by the ascendant Mbeki, who was installed as party president.

Still, despite Mandela's alienation from his erring and now former spouse, Winnie continued to be re-elected both to her party executive (achieving the top slot from the delegates in the National Executive Committee elections at the ANC 2007 conference) and to parliament, where she seldom if ever appeared.

There were, in fact, many sides to this complex and compelling woman. She was not simply a latter-day political gorgon, her criminal acts aside.

During a furious row with Mandela's successor, Mbeki, in early 2000 I was amazed to receive the following message from her on my voice mail: 'It's Winnie here – you really got to the president. Good luck to you.' And then, when my mother died in late 2001, she phoned me after the funeral to say, 'I'm so sorry, Tony, to hear of the death of your mother. I have only just heard about it now, otherwise I would have attended the funeral. I gather that your mother was a very strong woman and you must miss her terribly.'

Towards the end of his life, Mandela was reconciled with Winnie, an act apparently effected by his wife, Graça Machel, who appeared to the world, and by all accounts is, indeed, a person of probity and honour.

And then, in another tie that bound me further to both Winnie and Nelson Mandela, in the penultimate year of his life, in 2012, their elder daughter Zenani Mandela-Dlamini was appointed as my successor as South African ambassador to Argentina.

I did not meet Zenani before I left Buenos Aires in September of that year, although I gave her an extensive telephonic briefing on the post before I left it. But a few months later, when I was on a return visit on business to Argentina, we met for a cup of coffee in my favourite café in downtown Buenos Aires, the Florida Garden. She struck me as warm and, in the best sense of the word, ordinary and unaffected by the fame of her parents. At the beginning of our get-together she told me, 'Of course my mother sends you her special love.' I was stumped for a suitable reply.

Whatever Nelson Mandela's reasons for keeping his own counsel in respect of his wife and the political controversy I raised about her, I have to say I did not follow suit when, during his presidency, a member of my own family became a proxy target in the ANC's campaign of intended attrition against me.

CHAPTER SEVENTEEN

Relative Justice

AMANZIMTOTI, MEANING 'sweet waters' in isiZulu and so named, according to legend, by mighty King Shaka himself, is a rather ordinary coastal town some thirty kilometres outside my home city of Durban. Popular with some as a holiday destination, it also used to serve as a dormitory suburb for the metropole. It did little to excite attention or to attract much outside interest, except as a sign on the N2 national highway bypassed by visitors travelling to more alluring destinations further south.

All this changed two days before Christmas in 1985 when 'Toti', as locals called it, became an egregious synonym for the campaign of violence and terror the liberation movement brought into the heartland of white South Africa. Late on the afternoon of 23 December, when last-minute gift buyers and others thronged the shops, a young ANC operative, Andrew Zondo, made his way to the town's Sanlam shopping mall and placed a limpet mine in a bin just outside the centre. Shortly afterwards, using a remote device from some distance away, he detonated it. The blast killed five – two women and three children – and injured forty others, some seriously.

There was, of course, a bloody context to those times of intense struggle: the mid-1980s was a period of extreme violence as the state tightened its control and ANC guerrilla operatives intensified their response, hitting civilian targets ranging from Wimpy fast-food restaurants to recreational saloons. The infamous 1986 Magoo's Bar bombing on Durban's beachfront was a spectacular example.

The tit-for-tat violence reached its apogee months before the Toti blast when the SA Defence Force launched a cross-border raid into Gaborone in neighbouring Botswana, killing twelve, including family members of ANC exiles based there. Of course, 1985 was the year of President PW Botha's inglorious Rubicon speech – which, perversely, he declined to cross – signalling that protracted struggle, rather than a process of democratic negotiation, would mark the years ahead, as indeed it would for the remaining four years of his presidency.

A few months after Zondo was captured, he was charged with multiple counts of murder, and appeared before a judge and two assessors at the Scottburgh circuit court. The judge in question was my father, Ray, then in his nineteenth year as a provincial Supreme Court judge. South African law then obliged courts to impose a mandatory death sentence on convicted murderers, unless extenuating circumstances were proved. In the absence of such a finding, on 1 April 1986, my father sentenced Zondo to death. On appeal, the conviction and death sentence were upheld by the Appellate Division among whose number sat Justice Michael Corbett, who would preside as Chief Justice of South Africa at the beginning of Nelson Mandela's presidency. He was executed in September that year.

There were strands of irony here: my father regarded the conferring of the death sentence with a visceral dislike; he used to tell us that it made him 'physically ill' when he imposed it and thus, in more than two decades on the bench, he very rarely did so. After his retirement he became a leading campaigner for its abolition (which happened eventually in 1995). However, while on the bench he felt constrained to apply the law. But he also had established, through its creative use, a reputation as a determined liberal jurist. In a major case the year before the Zondo trial, for example, he delivered a landmark judgment, *Hurley v Minister of Law and Order*, which struck a decisive blow in favour of the liberty of detainees incarcerated by the security police. His decision to invalidate a detention order under the notorious section 29 of the Internal Security Act of 1982 was hailed as a major breakthrough by rights activists and scholars.[1]

Zondo became a *cause célèbre*, not simply because the ANC saw him as a martyr, but also because his fate assisted their demonisation of me (as in the case of my compulsory military service) and his death sentence would be inserted into debate continually throughout my political career. The attacks came from the low end to the very top of the party. An obscure ANC backbencher, for example, broke with the tradition of non-controversial maiden speeches to denounce me in 2006 as 'the son of an apartheid operative who ordered the execution of Andrew Zondo'.[2]

Shortly before the 1999 election campaign commenced, a more heavyweight member, Minister Nkosazana Dlamini-Zuma (today Chairperson of the African Union Commission) entered the lists on this issue in a parliamentary debate on the Truth Commission. 'The depth of our humanity,' she intoned with some immodesty, 'is illustrated by the fact that the judge who had the discretion to hang, or not to hang, a young revolutionary like Andrew Zondo is still a judge, and his progeny enjoys the direct fruit of the very freedom that Andrew died for.'[3]

Dlamini-Zuma was wrong on all counts: my father had long since retired; killing innocent shoppers in a suburban mall was questionable in terms of her own movement's proclaimed policy of the time; and the sentence imposed was mandatory, not discretionary. But, at least in this instance, she was not one to allow facts to interfere with her prejudices.

However, it was an earlier rendition of this mantra, or caricature, in the confines of the Gauteng province that led to my discussing directly with Nelson Mandela the use of my father and his conduct in judicial office as a means of attack on me. This early indicator of how the ANC conducted politics involved another member of my family, my elder brother, Peter.

Peter, who had established a flourishing legal practice in Johannesburg, had also been bitten by the political bug, which seemed to infect our whole family. His symptoms did not last as long as mine – he quit after 1999 – but in 1996 he was serving as party leader in the Gauteng provincial legislature. Given our small numbers at the time, he also doubled as spokesman on safety and security, which drew him into fierce political combat with the ANC provincial executive member for the portfolio, Jessie Duarte.

Duarte at the time had emerged as an ethically hobbled serial bungler in office.[4] Largely as a result of Peter's probing, aided by leaks from disgruntled members of her own administration, it was revealed that she had allegedly fabricated details of an accident involving her official motor vehicle to cover up the fact that she was driving it at the time, and without a licence. Then came revelations that she had ordered the province to pay for the travelling expenses of a male friend on an official overseas visit, even though he held no official title. Her son was subsequently also involved in the misuse of the official vehicle.

Interestingly, given the later ease with which state officials and politicians would abuse and plunder resources for their own ends, in those earlier times, at the onset of democratic government, some attempt was made, at certain times at least, to rein in the misuse of office. After Peter met the provincial premier, Dr Mathole Motshekga, he promptly appointed a commission of inquiry. It eventually reported that there 'were strong suspicions that [Duarte] had covered up the accident', and made other adverse findings against her. She was removed from political office and was 'rewarded' with a diplomatic posting.[5] (Duarte returned to high-profile politics during the Zuma presidency, and she currently serves as party deputy secretary general.)

It was early in Peter's war of political attrition with Duarte in 1996 that, stumped for an appropriate response to one of his probes in the legislature, she denounced him as 'the son of a hanging judge'. I saw this ploy as greatly problematic and, remembering that Duarte had once served as Mandela's secretary and that he had previously, notwithstanding the Zondo judgment, spoken of my father in the warmest terms, felt that I should seek the president's intervention.

I was mindful that, while I had indeed attacked his wife, Winnie, in a no-holds-barred fashion, she was a leading parliamentary and party politician in her own right. In any event, I had never sought to link Mandela to any of her controversies, and could not see how, on any basis of fundamental decency, the ANC could seek such a linkage in respect of my now retired father and his two politically active sons. I also felt most strongly that my father, a decent and honourable man, was having his reputation traduced as a means of scoring points against his children.

I had not disclosed to Mandela's office the reason for the requested appointment, which was set up for the early morning of Sunday in late September 1996. I was due to leave later that day for a visit to Israel, and my friend Cecil Bass, who was also active in the party, had volunteered to take me to the airport after my appointment with the president. He had offered to wait in the car outside Mandela's Houghton home while I conferred inside, but – sensing that he might enjoy an 'encounter with greatness', and being cognisant of the utility of having a witnessed conversation in such a matter – I invited him to come inside with me.

A security officer admitted us into the home, where we were greeted by a housekeeper who bustled upstairs to call Madiba. Shortly thereafter, he very slowly made his way down the staircase and, after greetings and introductions, explained he had undergone some medical procedure on his knee, which necessitated his being seated with his leg resting on an ottoman in the lounge. Cecil and I seated ourselves close by. After a brief discussion on the recently handed-down certification judgment of the Constitutional Court, I turned the conversation to the matter at hand. I had prepared carefully for this visit.

Very politely, I advised the president that I was 'dismayed' by the Duarte attack on my father, which had been amplified in recent days by remarks of Mandela's close friend, Durban sociologist Fatima Meer (who had written a very skewed account of the Zondo trial).

I asked Mandela to study a transcript of the actual judgment, that I handed over to him, having highlighted certain key paragraphs. These included the fact that Zondo, who had enjoyed excellent legal representation, per Denis Kuny SC, had not given evidence in the trial itself, but only on the question of extenuating circumstances. The evidence against him was given by a fellow ANC operative, his accomplice, whom the court found to be an 'excellent witness'. He had testified that the murders had been carefully planned and that, after the blast, Zondo had complained bitterly that 'only' five people had been killed. There was also evidence (not challenged in the trial) that he had acted contrary to the policy of the ANC not to target innocent civilians.

Before this meeting, I had closely questioned my father on whether Zondo's youth – he was just nineteen years old at the time – should not have mitigated the sentence. My father offered little comment, as was his wont in such matters, and asked me to read the judgment. The section on extenuating circumstances was also very heavily marked in the president's copy. It read:

> We live in a divided and troubled society, a society divided by differences and troubled by its failure to resolve them. The monopoly of power and its fruits rest in the hands of the white minority while the black majority are less affluent, voteless, and many live in conditions of squalor and degradation. It is against this background that this case must be judged. It has been held, quite rightly in my view, that youth, either alone or in conjunction with other circumstances, may be a factor operating in his favour. [The] youth of the accused must be a factor operating in his favour. Moreover, the accused did not commit his offence from base motives such as greed, or lust, or envy, but because he wished to help his people. That must also count in his favour.

On the other hand, there are matters which count against him, namely:

There has been unchallenged evidence that he acted against the clear policy of the ANC not to attack innocent civilians.

Not only did the accused express no remorse but he complained bitterly that only five people had been killed.[6]

Finally, the judgment moved on to the crime itself, where my father, noting that it was not an attack on a government building or the like, held:

What makes this crime so appalling is that it was committed against the civilian population as a whole. Young and old, black and white, innocent and guilty. Anyone shopping at the centre on Xmas eve was at risk of being killed.[7]

After noting that the onus of proving extenuating circumstances rests upon the accused, not upon the state, the court found that the onus had not been discharged and that such circumstances had 'not been proved to be present'.

Mandela read the judgment very carefully, and in silence. After he had finished reading, I suggested that, while I hardly expected him to agree with it, the judgment and my father's entire judicial record hardly portrayed him as 'an apartheid hanging judge' as some had recently suggested. I added that, if attacks on individual politicians were to be conducted via their familial links, there would be no end to the matter. I pointed out that his own father-in-law, (Winnie's parent) Columbus Madikizela, had served in the early homeland government of his cousin

Kaiser Matanzima in the Transkei, an early prop in the grand apartheid design. Mandela was somewhat bemused by this particular reference, but then addressed my central concern:

'There is no need to belabour the point,' he said. 'Once you start attacking the integrity of individuals there is indeed no end of the matter.' Anyway, he continued, 'the government's view on Judge Leon is quite different from that of one or two individuals'. He reminded me that, only a year or so before, the government had chosen my father to chair a high-level commission of inquiry into the Vaal Reefs mining disaster and that its wide-ranging report was a 'model' on which the state intended to base legislation for an overhaul of mining health and safety matters.[8]

Calling for his housekeeper to bring the telephone, he rang a no-doubt-surprised Cheryl Carolus, then deputy secretary general of the ANC, and summarised for her the purport of my visit. As Cecil recalled: 'He instructed her "pretty firmly" that this behaviour and these attacks had to stop, as they were "wrong" and "unfair".'

I was amazed at Mandela's approach – never having expected him to respond so affirmingly to a matter to which I simply wanted to draw to his attention. In fact, as the following years would reveal, in this small matter at least, Mandela's writ carried little weight, or the message was never delivered down the line.

Less than three months later, at my fortieth birthday celebrations, Mandela was seated next to my father. They had a warm discussion – but, to my knowledge, neither of them raised the question of the Zondo judgment.

CHAPTER EIGHTEEN

Road to Mafikeng

Mandela's presidential term would only end, formally at least, in mid-1999. But – in the real world of party power – he signalled its political closure in August 1997, shortly after his seventy-ninth birthday. His announcement that he would relinquish the leadership of the ANC at its next national conference in December in the town of Mafikeng in North West province, near the country's border with Botswana, was the prelude to his stepping down as president eighteen months later.

Doubtless, in so doing, Mandela was aware of the eternal truth of Pompey's much-quoted saying to Sully, 'More men worship the rising than the setting sun'. Political eyes had shifted increasingly to his deputy president and anointed successor, Thabo Mbeki. Under Mandela, Mbeki had effectively been running the administration in the detailed implementation – and sometimes non-implementation – of policy, a de facto prime minister in all but title. But he lacked many of Mandela's key attributes: the heroic record and the generosity of spirit, the personal ease and the sure touch with the grand gesture. Mandela's successor was the polar opposite to his famed openness – secretive and suspicious of any views and voices outside his close circle of allies, largely drawn from the world of exile politics that he had inhabited for most of his adult life.

It was precisely Mandela's highly unusual combination of qualities that allowed him to soar solo in the political stratosphere, while all other local politicians, and most of his international peers, flew far below him in the cumulus clouds. Mbeki could, certainly before assuming the highest office and even in the early stages of his presidency, rely on Mandela's support and affirmation. Any mistakes Mbeki made, as one of Mandela's admiring biographers, Mike Nicol, described the now-accelerating transition from the one to the other, '[would] be absorbed by the dazzling Mandela shield'.[1]

But, well before his formal announcement, the atmospherics of reconciliation fashioned by Mandela risked being sullied by an altogether more fissile element in the ANC's political chemistry: strident racism.

It was perhaps appropriate that ANC firebrand Tony Yengeni gave early warning of the shift: in March 1996 he told parliament that whites had accumulated their wealth by stealing from blacks.[2] Yengeni would later be convicted of and jailed for defrauding parliament in regard to a kickback he received from one of the suppliers in the controversial Arms Deal, which he had ardently championed. This was of a piece with Jacob Zuma's attempt to defend his maladroit then-wife Nkosazana Dlamini-Zuma for her public squandering of monies on the *Sarafina II* debacle, by saying she would not have been attacked had she been white.[3]

By the time the ANC met in Mafikeng in December 1997 for its watershed 50th National Conference, the legislative process for the re-racialisation of South Africa was mostly in place. Both laws and executive practice had by then decreed that 'racial demographics' would be determinative in public sector appointments and, increasingly, be a requirement for private sector companies as well. However, there apparently existed a consensus of party opinion that white South Africans needed a wake-up call, and that 'Mandela was the man to deliver it'.[4]

SABC TV thoughtfully arranged for its viewers to watch Mandela's address to the conference live. I began observing proceedings early on the morning of 16 December before wending my way to a wedding. When I returned home from the happy nuptials and a splendid lunch, I was amazed to see Mandela still on the platform delivering his speech. It was a marathon four-and-a-half-hour address, interrupted by a meal break.

Mafikeng was not simply to be a changing of the guard between Mandela and Mbeki – the latter elected unopposed as ANC president and therefore the man who would incontestably become the next national president after the general election eighteen months hence. It was also to set the seal on and draw together all the strands of the race agenda, which had by then, alongside the fading reconciliation championed by Mandela, become the predominant feature of South African public and political life.

By the time it gathered for the Mafikeng conference, the ANC was unquestionably in control of South Africa. The largest opposition grouping, the NP, was in the process of rapid disintegration. Little had come of the much-threatened right-wing revolt against black rule, and, despite occasional squeals, the government enjoyed wide support from previous opposition bastions such as the English-speaking press and the universities.

Mandela's address was in its own fashion unprecedented and revealing. Gone was the gentle national conciliator and the emblem of South Africa's rainbow aspirations. Apparently Mbeki and his intellectual alter ego, Joel Netshitenzhe, wrote the speech – or were much involved in its drafting. It was clearly good politics from an internal point of view to suggest that the Mbeki age of transformation had the blessing of Mandela, and the president certainly lived up to this requirement. He gave clear notice that the heights that the ANC commanded across politics and much of civil society were insufficient for the party's appetite.

Yet, since the ANC held such a predominant position, he nonetheless had to conjure up some ghosts and phantasms to make it clear that the organisation, far from being secure, was in fact under some kind of threat.

He turned his attack bare-fistedly on the opposition, claiming somewhat risibly that the 'National Party has not abandoned its strategic objective of the total destruction of our organisational movement ... [and] is involved in a desperate search to find the ways and means to destroy its historic enemy [the ANC]'.[5]

Of course, I was not unduly sympathetic to his enemy, which was also my own. But I was staggered when he went on to accuse the DP and NP of engaging in 'a desperate struggle ... to convince the white minority that they are the most reliable and best defenders of white privilege'.[6]

Nor did 'the bulk of the mass media' – as Mandela chose to characterise what I actually regarded as a fawning press – escape his wrath. Their crime? Setting themselves up, in Mandela's words, 'as [a] force opposed to the ANC ... to campaign against both real change and the real agents of change, as represented by our movement'.[7]

While Mandela's speech caused some concern and grabbed the head-lines, it was immediately discounted by many as simply addressing an internal audience, placating some of the wilder ANC elements in order to gain their endorsement of the macro-economic approach embodied in the GEAR document. This immediately led ANC-inclined sympa-thisers to play down the rhetoric as being of less importance than the economic substance.

Overseas commentators were less forgiving in their analysis than most of the local press. The *Daily Telegraph* dubbed it a 'depressingly para-noid tirade' and *The Independent* was sharply critical in its denunciation: 'meaningless dogma ... antiquated gibberish'. From left-field, even *The Observer* was constrained to call out the great man for his 'profoundly depressing assault'.[8] When asked for comment, I, who generally – both due to personal regard and for reasons of political probity – was wary of criticising Mandela personally, described his marathon remarks, with some accuracy, as 'the low-water mark of his presidency'.

But those who assumed that the surrender of socialism meant the abandonment of the party's national revolutionary agenda were mis-taken. A scholar of this period later pointed out in his careful analysis of Mafikeng that 'the ANC simply sought a racial rather than a socialist transformation of South Africa'.[9]

The resolutions that flew out of the conference included a demand for even more rapid affirmative action focused primarily on black people, and called for the South African National Defence Force and the Police Service to be made even more demographically representative.

The Mafikeng conclave followed on a seminal decision some six weeks before. At a Tripartite Alliance summit in October, the movement outlined a plan to capture the state in its entirety. A key document – 'The State, Property Relations and Social Transformation' – explicitly rejected the idea that the state should be 'a neutral non-partisan entity'. It endorsed the notion that the state was 'an instrument in the hands of the liberation movement'. It also affirmed and embraced the Leninist notion of crushing the old order 'to extend the power of the national liberation movement over all levers of power: the army, the police, the bureaucracy, intelligence structures, the judiciary, parastatals, and agencies such as regulatory bodies, the public broadcaster, the central bank and so on'.[10]

By November 1998 the ANC National Working Committee established a National Deployment Committee, headed by Jacob Zuma, and adopted a strategy for the employment of ANC cadres in all areas of government and society that 'the movement regarded as crucial for the transformation of the project'. Now only the police remained outside the control of the party, in the sense that its head, Commissioner George Fivaz, was not yet of the party faithful. This was to change in January 2000 when Jackie Selebi, a former ANC MP and diplomat, was made commissioner, despite having no police background. His unfitness for this office was to be revealed, starkly, some years hence; in July 2010, he was convicted on multiple charges of corruption, involving a drug lord, and sentenced to fifteen years in jail.

The non-racial prospectus of the Freedom Charter that 'South Africa belongs to all who live in it, black and white' was no longer sufficient for the ANC: proportion of population was what really mattered – along with ANC party membership.

I still held the view that Mandela himself, although undoubtedly responsible for the major events at the conference and for the speech he delivered at it, should be judged for the many things he had got right. Therefore, in the next parliamentary State of the Nation debate after Mafikeng, in February 1998, I tried to reconcile Mandela's universally – and correctly – acclaimed decency with his stance at the party's National Conference. 'His moral stature may not be in doubt,' I said, 'but his political judgment may well be. To stamp us [the DP] as part of some dire conspiratorial web hell bent on destabilising the new order in South Africa beggars the imagination ... [The] depiction of opponents of the ANC as racist enemies of transformation determined to sabotage our fragile democratic order is a sinister attempt to stifle dissent and distort debate. This, Mr President, is a journey down a populist blind alley ... You do not build democracy upon the delegitimisation of your opponents; you do not cement freedoms by excoriating the media; you do not bind the wounds of our suffering nation with a populist band-aid.'[11]

Mandela, whose regard for parliament was considerable and whose enjoyment of lively debate was often evident in his engagement with it, chose not to respond to this entreaty when he answered the debate.

Parliamentary rhetoric was one thing, but the DP needed to document the risk of the Rainbow Nation's succumbing to something darker. We launched one of our most controversial pamphlets as a response to the post-Mafikeng situation, entitling it 'The Death of the Rainbow Nation: Unmasking the ANC's Programme of Re-racialisation'.[12] Our seventy-five-page document, authored by ace party researcher James Myburgh, today editor of the influential website Politicsweb, sought to explain how the ANC had moved in three years from a vision of South Africa as a society – in Mandela's words – 'inspiringly united around the commitment to a common future' to one of racial division.

The policy malaise was located in the misconception that the advancement of blacks and minorities was mutually exclusive, and that opportunities were finite. Government white papers and affirmative action policies assumed that demographic representivity was synchronous with equality. Yet affirmative action did little to improve the lot of the poorest. Indeed, race-based affirmative action was the flipside of race discrimination: for everyone being discriminated against, someone else was being affirmed.

The document, which was highly contested within the party (a parliamentary colleague referred to it as 'the death document'), drew attention to the fact that racial bean-counting had become so pervasive in government departments that massive numbers of crucial posts were left vacant when the only people qualified to apply for them were white. The same government departments were simply re-engaging as expensive consultants those who had left with golden handshakes.

One ANC politician, Firoz Cachalia, called our report 'a crude apology for apartheid'. The DP's attempts to draw attention to the shortcomings of racial transformation 'amounted … to a demand that nothing be done to fully address the imbalances which existed'.[13]

Much could be done, and we could point to various policies involving skills training, opportunity vouchers, and the like; but, as I indicated in a response to Cachalia: 'Race makes good politics but it too often leads to bad policies because it provides the policymakers with an excuse to avoid the really difficult problems.'[14]

The fact is, Mandela's personality, and his presidency, was a living embodiment of these lines from Walt Whitman's famous poem 'Song of Myself' – 'Do I contradict myself? / Very well then I contradict myself,

(I am large, I contain multitudes.)' – and he more or less brushed off Mafikeng and continued to champion his more generous vision of what he wanted his country to become.

As it happened, an episode that occurred shortly after his opening address to parliament in 1998 seemed at first blush to suggest that elements of the old order were seeking to discredit the new. This was the so-called Meiring Plot involving an intelligence report handed to the president by Chief of the Defence Force General Georg Meiring. It suggested that a group of black leaders, including Winnie Mandela, Bantu Holomisa and Magoo's Bar bomber Robert McBride (for which he later received an amnesty from the TRC), were, among other things, 'planning to promote chaos in order to seize power after the 1999 elections'. It also suggested that senior black officers were 'unfit to command', and fingered in this regard Siphiwe Nyanda, a former ANC military commander, and the person identified as the next Defence Chief.[15]

Mandela was suspicious on receiving the report, not so much of its contents, which he eventually discounted, but more of its provenance. He did not denounce it outright, but, in a crab-like, though impeccable, manner, went about deconstructing it: he appointed Chief Justice Ismail Mahomed to head a judicial commission to interrogate its validity. The judges found that the report was 'without substance', and Meiring was bundled out into early retirement.[16]

To be sure, there were other elements from the old order who found it difficult to accommodate themselves to the change of power, and their loss of it. A prime exemplar of this tendency was the rugby boss Dr Louis Luyt, a hectoring bully (with whom I would later have a brief and unhappy political association). Despite Mandela's *Invictus* moments in the 1995 Rugby World Cup, Luyt intensely resented government attempts to transform and deracialise South African rugby, and its appointment of a commission of inquiry into Luyt's conduct of rugby affairs.

There certainly were legitimate reasons to oppose the ANC's attempts to control all elements of society, including sport. But Luyt did not content himself with using the judicial process to do so. His legal team and the trial judge William de Villiers in March 1998 subpoenaed the president to testify in court personally. In typical fashion, although Mandela told the media before taking the stand that 'his blood boiled at being forced into court' – the first president ever obliged so to defend an executive decision – he did so 'out of respect for the administration of justice'. The court, headed by an old order jurist, ultimately found in Luyt's favour and against Mandela. But the wider point was far more important: the president upheld judicial processes, even those that went against him.

And, while the exceptions, such as Mafikeng, were often as revealing and important as the general thrust of Mandela's leadership, it remains incontestable that as president he transcended the narrow partisan and racial divisions of South Africa. His successor, however, as Mbeki's ill-starred presidency would show, tended to reinforce them.

CHAPTER NINETEEN

Leaving

AGED JUST FORTY-ONE in July 1998, I had limited experience of attending eightieth birthday celebrations. But the bash arranged for Nelson Mandela's big day was perhaps like no other for anyone of any age.

On his actual birthday – 18 July – at a private ceremony at his Houghton home, he had married Graça Machel, his sweetheart of recent years. Graça, the widow of Mozambique President Samora Machel, thus became the first woman in the world to have been wed to two different heads of state. She was an admired figure of immense rectitude, and, while lacking the glamour and beauty of Winnie, she also had none of the latter's infamy. Samora and Graça Machel had been leading figures in the liberation of their country from Portuguese colonialism. Conspiracy theorists were, even at the time of her marriage to Mandela, convinced that President Machel's October 1986 death in a plane crash on the South African border with Mozambique was a consequence of the dirty

195

tricks of the apartheid regime. However, a more likely cause (buttressed by a judicial commission of inquiry that included international aviation experts) was the error – possibly caused by drunkenness – of the Russian pilots at the Tupolev TU-134's controls.

This was all quite distant in 1998 when, on the night after Mandela's actual birthday, some two thousand of us gathered in the sumptuous pavilions of Gallagher Estate – midway between Johannesburg and Pretoria – to celebrate Madiba's marriage and his eightieth birthday. The 'usual suspects' of South Africa's political elite, among whose number I was counted, were all present, but we were merely bit players in an event whose star power could barely have been equalled at any other such gathering.

Stevie Wonder was at the keyboard to lead us in singing 'Happy Birthday' to the world's most famous octogenarian, and at the table next to mine – seated in a wheelchair – was a frail Nina Simone, the famed US jazz singer and civil rights activist. Then, making a very late and appropriately dramatic entrance, and surrounded by more bodyguards than even the president, Michael Jackson entered, a study in artificial pallor and major weirdness.

But none of the international celebrities detracted an iota from the most famed man in the room, Mandela himself. Eighty children lit each of the candles on his giant cake, and he danced the famed Madiba jive to the accompaniment of the band. His remarks commenced with a phrase he had seldom used since his release from jail nearly a decade before, 'My wife and I ...' It was met by thunderous applause from us all.

The only off-key note of the evening, or so I thought, was the preceding toast to the bridal couple delivered by Thabo Mbeki. Never particularly at ease at such mega-events, he chose (of all the texts available from the opus of the Bard) to quote at length from *King Lear*. Whether consciously or not, Mbeki's choice on such a happy and star-saturated night of a tragedy that highlights brutality, loss of power and ingratitude towards a retired regent was more than passing strange.

Mandela's presidency now had less than a year to run. Ever more than before, he detached himself from the petty urgencies and exigencies of daily governance and travelled the country and the wider world sticking to the big themes – nation-building and reconciliation and social justice – on which he had elaborated during his eight years of freedom.

On its final sitting day before the June elections, parliament convened on Friday 26 March 1999 in a special session to bid its founding democratic president a fond farewell. Since the passing of the constitution in 1996 and the repeal of all apartheid legislation, much of the recent activity in the House had been more concerned with state power and pageantry, in almost inverse proportion to its serious work as a legislature. Political debates had also been characterised by an increasingly rancorous, often crude name-calling tone.

Aptly, Mandela's leave-taking from parliament was as inclusive and joyous as his presidency had been. Many years later, the Speaker of that era, Dr Frene Ginwala, remarked that Mandela always wore a (very well-cut) suit to parliament in place of his trademark batik-style shirts, one of which he even wore to a formal banquet at Buckingham Palace. 'He was determined to uphold the dignity of the House', she recalled.[1] This he had always done, and not just in his sartorial choices when in attendance.

Each party leader now had an opportunity to pay tribute to this remarkable president, notionally an opponent, but so much more than that, something very difficult to express in words.

Aided by a speech to which my part-time speech writer, Andrew Kenny, had added some sparkling prose, I was privileged to participate. My public tribute was a sincere attempt to express not only what the party and I thought of him, but what we genuinely believed he had done for our nation:

> There are three categories of great political leaders. The first is the great and the bad: this includes Hitler and Stalin. The second is the great and the good: this includes Winston Churchill and Franklin Roosevelt. And then there is a third category, also of good, but of a leader born with a special kind of grace, who seems to transcend the politics of his age. This is a very small category, and in fact I can think of only three such men in this century: Mahatma Gandhi, the Dalai Lama and Nelson Mandela.[2]

Mandela, I went on, had managed 'to raise the sights of our politics ... We see how he was that rarest phenomenon – a committed politician and an unusually agreeable and generous man ... I am deeply honoured that I have been able to see from these benches the ending of apartheid and the beginning of full democracy under the presidency of Nelson Mandela. My respect and admiration for him is unconditional. He graces this House. He graces this country. He graces humanity.'[3]

I went down from the podium and we shook hands very warmly; I shed a tear at taking formal leave of this extraordinary phenomenon. At one level he was all too human, but at another he inhabited a plane out of reach of most mortal politicians. It had been a great gift that my political leadership had commenced under his presidency and had grown, not under his enormous shadow, but because of that special light that he shone on so many, including me.

My sadness at taking leave of Mandela was also occasioned by a fore-taste of what was to follow. A few months before the June election, I had arranged to meet Mandela's successor, Mbeki, at his office in the Union Buildings in Pretoria.

The purpose of the meeting was mundane: after Zach de Beer had resigned his ambassadorship in 1996, I had successfully arranged with Mandela for a DP provincial legislator, Western Cape educationist Professor Richard van der Ross, to receive a foreign posting (as ambassa-dor to Spain). Now another political colleague had expressed an interest in an ambassadorship. (At the time, I thought the job essentially routine and boring, a sort of glorified town mayor's role with little real power, though, in later years, I would change my mind.) My intention was to ask Mbeki whether the informal foreign posting arrangement reached with Mandela would continue. Van der Ross's term would expire on Mbeki's watch.

In marked contrast to our previous encounters when at all times Mbeki had been warm and welcoming, on this occasion he was distinctly cold. Mbeki suggested that, if any DP MPs wished to be considered, they should 'join the Department of Foreign Affairs' and enter the public service.

That disposed of my central concern. I then added conversationally that, in respect of the coming election, we should 'keep the channels of communication open' in case there was one or other matter requiring resolution (I had in mind the chaotic events that had characterised the 1994 elections). Mbeki responded curtly that the Independent Electoral Commission (IEC) would handle matters properly. The ease and affabil-ity of the past had vanished.

Driving back to Johannesburg, I pondered the change that Mbeki had undergone, which would mark his presidency. There was no easy explanation, but the warmth and frequent contact that had characterised my relationship with Mandela would not continue with his successor. And if, as I hoped – as the results confirmed – the electorate conferred on me the leadership of the opposition, our relationship with the president would be determined by him, and not by me, as a supplicant, seeking crumbs of relevance from his table of power.

I never – contrary to various fabulists in the media who suggested otherwise – sought another meeting with Mbeki over the next eight years, save until a few days before my retirement from party leadership in May 2007.

Given his attitude to me, unignorable on that day, the lights were on but no one was at home. I was hardly alone in experiencing the chill winds from the president-in-waiting. His years in the highest office were to be characterised by an extreme remoteness, which was to lead to his unseating before he could complete his second term as president. As many of his one-time allies became his deadliest opponents, I was convinced that, for such a proclaimed lover of Shakespeare, he had clearly never read the portion of *King Henry IV Part II,* where, on his assumption of the kingdom, Prince Hal turns to his old friend and mentor Falstaff, and chillingly repudiates him: 'Presume not that I am the thing I was; / For God doth know, so the world shall perceive, / That I have turn'd away my former self ...'

Fairly early on in the Mbeki era, even his famed mentor would feel the icy blast that emanated from his successor.

CHAPTER TWENTY

Twilight

JOHANNESBURG STOCKBROKER Sidney Frankel was hardly alone in the ranks of the South African business community in switching support from the National Party, as the *ancien régime's* grip on power was loosened, to the new political elite of the African National Congress. He certainly wasn't embarrassed about showing off his fraternalism in some style, as I was to discover soon after the hard-fought June 1999 election.

The campaign had propelled my party from the peripheral flanks of opposition politics to the status of official opposition (the second-largest party in parliament, supplanting the National Party in the process, but way behind the governing ANC, which increased its majority in the poll). I was both thrilled by the result and exhausted by the process of obtaining it. So an invitation to hobnob with Frankel and his clients in the luxury of his private game reserve seemed an agreeable pit stop before the parliamentary session commenced.

I was also aware that our controversial and successful campaign, which quintupled the party vote, had excited frissons of disapproval within the ANC and its media supporters, and doubtless among some in the business community as well. We had campaigned under the slogan 'Fight Back' – dreamt up by our US political consultants based on local focus groups, and an unambiguous reference to the party's resolve to confront the crime and corruption that had manifested itself across the country in the preceding few years of ANC government. But the ANC, despite the deliberately non-racial nature of our campaign, had immediately dubbed it 'Fight Black'. This stigma-label was to cast a long pall over the next phase of politics – although, as events would reveal, it was Mbeki who would place race front and centre of the country's politics and his administration's policies.

Our first post-election decision, in keeping with our mandate of increasing opposition-aligned provincial governments, was to form a coalition with the Nationalists in the Western Cape, where our party held the balance of power between the New National Party, as the Nationalists had rebranded themselves, and the ANC. This had been denounced by the ANC, and some business leaders – of whom it might be said they had never met a government they did not like, whether National or African National. Against this background, the Frankel-sponsored shindig in the game reserve also seemed a good place to defend our decision.

Our group included Bantu Holomisa, whose United Democratic Movement (UDM) had obtained a sliver of seats in the election (though fewer than half of our total of thirty-eight MPs). Frankel assembled us in the *boma* (enclosure) in the middle of the rather rustic but well-appointed guest chalets dotted around the lodge.

We were essentially a supporting cast for the arrival, heralded by the throbbing approach of an Air Force helicopter, of the star attraction of the weekend: the recently retired president Mandela. He duly ambled from the landing area, and the suitably enthralled guests enjoyed their close-up time with global celebrity. Mandela and I had a brief but inconsequential chat; he did not refer to the recent election (in which he had starred at the ANC's final rally) or to my new status in the body politic, but offered a few jokes in his address about 'Mickey Mouse parties' in which number, alongside me and my party, he included his old protégé and now nemesis, Holomisa.

But the Disneyesque banter, which, with some exceptions chronicled in this book, had characterised my largely warm relationship with Mandela, did not – as my pre-election meeting with Mbeki foretold – transfer itself to the new president. Acid, rather than spoonfuls of sugar, would characterise this relationship.

I suppose that the very long shadow cast by a famed predecessor can wrong-foot even the surest political operator when he ascends to power. Recent political history offered many such sobering successions: Georges Pompidou after Charles de Gaulle, John Major succeeding Margaret Thatcher, and George HW Bush taking the baton from Ronald Reagan were three sad and salutary examples, and Gordon Brown's beleaguered premiership, post-Tony Blair, would provide another in the future.

But Mbeki added his own attributes to the problem of inheriting the crown from a universally admired and loved figure, who, as the *Sunday Times* had once noted, was 'Teflon coated'. Mbeki, in contrast, was 'Velcro Man' – all his mistakes stuck to him. In fact, in a lesser noted speech at the 1997 Mafikeng conference, rather than the lengthy address for which I, and others, had roasted him, Mandela clearly intuited some of these personality traits. Although Mandela couched his remarks in the claim that 'our President [Mbeki] understands these issues', the departing leader's words were plain enough, and events would prove them to be eerily prophetic:

> One of the temptations of a leader who has been elected unopposed [Mbeki's election to the party presidency was unanimous] is that he may use that powerful position to settle scores with his detractors. He may marginalize them and, in certain cases, get rid of them and surround himself with yes-men and women. His first duty is to allay the concerns of his colleagues in the leadership, for them to be able to discuss freely without fear within the internal structures of the movement. Any subject should be discussed from all angles and people should even be able to criticize the leader without fear or favour.[1]

However coded or otherwise Mandela intended his warning to be, Mbeki's presidency proceeded to move in exactly the opposite direction.

As leader of the opposition in Mbeki's new parliament, I was often left open-mouthed at how many hostages the president gifted to his opponents. By June 2000, Mbeki and I had become embroiled in a heated and voluminous dispute over his refusal to provide anti-retroviral drugs (ARVs) to HIV/AIDS victims, and, by then, he had set himself up as perhaps the most powerful and infamous AIDS-denialist in the world. Our own correspondence on the subject ran to over a hundred pages and revealed a president who had not only succumbed to believing fringe opinion on the subject, but, at ruinous cost to the lives of his citizens, had now mandated this position as state policy.

Of course, Mbeki was little troubled, or did not affect to be, by the displeasure of his political opponents, civil society and – over time – the domestic judiciary (but to be fair, he did abide by the Constitutional Court judgment on the provision of ARVs), which overruled the government on the issue, or even world opinion. But he was forced to retaliate when no less a figure than Mandela decided to enter the lists on the controversy.

As it happened, for much of Mandela's presidency, the pandemic was neglected, a fact later acknowledged by Mandela himself on several occasions, such as when he disclosed that his own son Makgatho had died of an AIDS-related illness in January 2005. Official neglect, during the Mandela presidency, reinforced the wall of silence surrounding the syndrome.

There were issues of social and cultural taboo that made it difficult, apparently even for a head of state, to discuss a sexually transmitted disease openly and candidly. The main vector of transmission was heterosexual intercourse – a topic not often discussed in public. The Calvinist and Victorian sensibilities of the white population, combined with the traditional patriarchal values of many black communities, cast a shadow over public discourse, leaving the victims of HIV/AIDS in a shroud of shame and loneliness.

But I was to witness personally how, after stepping down from the presidency, Mandela made up for lost time, speaking out about the disease and even, implicitly, against some of the unhelpful policies of his successor in dealing with it. Nonetheless, it needs to be noted that Mandela's years in office were the period in which HIV/AIDS took root and spread exponentially through the population.

I was in the audience at the Mount Nelson Hotel in Cape Town in February 2002, when, at a Henry J Kaiser Family Foundation function, Mandela gave an extraordinary explanation for the neglect of AIDS on his watch. In his frank manner, he said that, when he was first released from jail and started campaigning, he had preached the gospel of condom use and spoken of the perils of AIDS. However, on a visit to a school once, he was admonished by a teacher who warned that, if he persisted, 'no one will vote for you'. This semi-apologia was coupled to a slightly veiled but stinging criticism of his successor's strange policies and overall inaction. He pointedly stated, for example, 'At least I am willing to admit when I have made a mistake.' Later it became known that the issue led to an almost complete breakdown in his personal relationship with Mbeki.

Just how badly their partnership had deteriorated was not, at first, known to me or others outside ANC party structures. However, soon enough it was revealed that Mandela had been humiliated by Mbeki's lieutenants when, a month or so after his Mount Nelson speech, Mandela had decided to exercise his right as a member of the party's national executive to plead with it to change course, and to provide ARVs, particularly to the most at-risk categories of rape victims, pregnant women and health workers. One of his biographers, Martin Meredith, citing eyewitness accounts, described the meeting in painful detail:

> Mbeki's response [to Mandela's intervention] was characteristically vindictive ... As Mbeki looked on silently, one member after another stood up to abuse Mandela for breaking party discipline, vying with each other to deride him in order to curry favour with Mbeki. According to one witness, Ngoako Ramatlhodi, they were like a 'pack

of wild dogs tearing their prey' – 'wild, aggressive and merciless.' Only two members defended Mandela's right to speak out. 'After his vicious mauling', said Ramatlhodi, 'Madiba looked twice his age, old and ashen'. The NEC [National Executive Committee] went on to decide not to provide antiretroviral drugs to pregnant women, rape victims or health workers because the drugs 'remained unproven'.[2]

Mandela later recounted this saga to me (and doubtless to many others as well) and said he was saddened by the NEC's closure of the culture of party debate, and he went forth with a domestic and international campaign, drawing attention to the disease, its causes and, in crucial contrast to the parallel world now inhabited by Mbeki, its effective treatment.

If neglect marked Mandela's tenure, denial stamped Mbeki's. There was no initial attempt at prevention and treatment, and Mbeki actively questioned the link between HIV and AIDS – exaggerating the toxicity of ARVs. He and his health minister espoused a spectrum of heterodox theories and outright quackery, resisting the findings of Western medicine and science, and the research of pharmaceutical companies, essentially on the basis of misconceived national and racial pride.

Doctors who attempted to prescribe ARVs – the only clinically effective treatment for HIV/AIDS – were occasionally punished, while non-governmental organisations that attempted to provide the drugs as prophylactics to rape victims were evicted from government hospitals.

The debates and confrontations erupting around these events and Mbeki's denialist stance caused severe damage to the president's personal reputation and the international standing of the country. South Africa's HIV/AIDS policy became a synonym for disaster. Ironically, it was

Mbeki's much-criticised (often for good reason) successor, Jacob Zuma, who, lacking any of the intellectual pretensions or racial hang-ups of his predecessor, restored South African HIV/AIDS policy to a position of admired normality, basing it on medical science and removing it, finally, from the arena of public contestation.

In fact, the issue of HIV/AIDS and another early misstep in the Mbeki era – dealing (or, more accurately, temporising) with the tyrant across the Limpopo, Robert Mugabe of Zimbabwe – were the consequence of the new president's viewing every major policy challenge through the distorting prism of race. Thus any focus on the transmission of HIV became, from Mbeki's explicit perspective, a result of 'minds who have been corrupted by the disease of racism … [according to which] we are portrayed as oversexed or lascivious … rampant sexual beasts, unable to control our urges …' as he subsequently assailed (white) opposition MP Ryan Coetzee, who dared to ask him whether the widespread prevalence[3] of rape could, in part, account for the spread of HIV.

Basic truths, such as standing up for a sensible public health policy or for democracy in Africa, had a very hard swim in the waters made mephitic by the issue of race and the president's determination to allow it to trump every other aspect of public debate.

Given that Mbeki was now taking on international opinion and increasingly moving against the grain of the hitherto quiescent local media and influence-shapers, especially in the ranks of civil society and the trade unions, his presidency began to assume an almost belea-guered atmosphere and a bunker-like defensiveness, despite the ruling party's impregnable political position. The most obvious and disturbing early warning of the politics of suspicion now occupying the summit of government arose in May 2001. Mbeki's ultra-loyal and hard-drinking safety and security minister, Steve Tshwete, mumbled (his normal manner of speech) on television news that there was 'a plot against the president'. This was apparently based on the statement of an ANC operative in Mpumalanga that Mbeki was somehow complicit in the assassination of Chris Hani in 1993.

The rumour had done the rounds on an almost continuous basis right through to 2007, but now Tshwete identified the three members who were behind this apparent plot: Cyril Ramaphosa, Tokyo Sexwale and Mathews Phosa, three ANC heavyweights, each of whom had in varying degrees fallen out with Mbeki.

Even the normally docile South African media sat up and took notice.

However, the local reaction (largely one of incredulity) was nothing compared with the denting of Mbeki's image overseas. *The Economist*, for example, headlined an editorial: 'Mbeki loses the plot ... And South Africa finds it has a paranoid president'. It wondered, in fact, whether the outing of the plotters did not mean that Mbeki was going off the rails. It stated, '[But] Mr Mbeki is not barmy, merely paranoid. That, at least, seems the most likely explanation of the conspiracy episode. How comforting that should be to South Africans is another matter.'[4]

Mandela shortly thereafter rose to the defence of the three, and the 'plot' was revealed to contain no substance. It indicated that the presidency considered itself under siege, this time not from 'white politicians', as Mbeki was subsequently to refer to me, but from a fifth column within.

Over the next eighteen months I was immersed in fusing together a united opposition under the banner of the Democratic Alliance, which comprised the Democratic Party and the New National Party. Its first outing at the polls, in the December 2000 local government elections, proved it to be very successful, with opposition voters obtaining over 23 per cent of the vote. But it was a marriage of both unequal and incompatible partners and, within eighteen months of its formation, the NNP leadership deserted the party to make common cause with its historic enemy, the ANC.

The schism, in which Mbeki and his top command played a significant role, allowed our opponents to paint the Democratic Alliance in false colours – reactionary and out of step with the new political *Zeitgeist*, allegedly now represented by the governing party and its new-found ally. I was determined to push back against this caricature, and also to seek wise counsel on whether a proper working relationship could be forged between government and the official opposition, which I had now been leading for nearly two years. During this entire period a deep freeze had set in between government and our party, the largest opposition bloc in parliament.

It seemed to me that Mandela himself, the exemplar of a president who simultaneously relished partisan politics and engaging in frequent contact with his opponents, might have some answers in this regard.

Thus I found myself in September 2002 back in a very familiar locale: the Houghton residence of the ex-president. Madiba evinced the warmth and bonhomie of old, although he seemed much aged since he had relinquished office just over three years before.

On the matter of my enquiry, his response was astonishing; he laughed and told me, 'Thabo is much too busy to take my calls or to see me these days.' When I expressed some astonishment at this rejoinder, he reached into a pile of newspapers close to hand and with some amusement drew my attention to a *Mail & Guardian* cartoon dated 25 January 2001 from the corrosive pen of master cartoonist Zapiro. It consisted of an elaborate organogram depicting the imagined presidential office structure of Mbeki. One of its panels represented the 'Don't Mention Madiba Committee'. The point was quite plain. I then asked Mandela if, given the depths to which government–opposition relations had now sunk, he had any practical advice as to how they might be restored in an effective fashion. His response was equally bewildering: 'You must seek the advice of JZ – he's the key man in the party and the government.'

I thought this indicated that Mandela was really out of touch. He was referring to Jacob Zuma, the deputy president, who cut an amiable figure in parliament but had been widely discounted as a real power player at the time, or even into the future. Indeed, some months before, he had been humiliatingly obliged by the Mbeki guardians to issue a bizarre statement that he had no interest in becoming president, and afterwards a suicide letter from his wife had mysteriously been leaked to the newspapers. But, as events would prove, Mandela in fact knew better than most where the future power in his movement lay.

One further surprise awaited me that day. My meeting request with Mandela had, as per my fashion in these matters, been treated by my office as a private one, from which we sought no publicity. But the former president had other ideas. As our discussion drew to a close, he urged me to accompany him to the outside veranda. Awaiting us there was a phalanx of reporters and photographers. Mandela then put his arm around my shoulder and told the gathering, 'Tony Leon is a proper democrat and there should be dialogue at all levels of our country.' I assumed he was really aiming his message at his successor, but was grateful, at a very difficult political time, for his strong encouragement.

Mandela also used this press briefing to call for 'negotiations' to try to clear the looming war clouds then gathering over Saddam Hussein's Iraq. Our meeting coincided with US President George W Bush's address to the United Nations, in which he demanded world action against the 'grave and gathering danger' of Iraq and threatened unilateral action if the world body declined to act.[5] The conflict would animate Mandela to denounce the US President.

For me, the next period in our politics was characterised by rebuilding the opposition project after the desertion of the NNP and preparing for the next general election in April 2004, which saw my party increase its support but, again, be dwarfed by Mbeki's ANC.

As it happens, my opening salvo in the 2004 election was provided by Mandela himself. The previous July he had apparently raised – and promptly discounted – the spectre of Mbeki seeking a third term in office (the constitution limited presidents to two five-year terms). He made the reservation, however, in the crab-like manner in which he always approached matters relating to Mbeki, declaring: 'Not the Mbeki I know. He could not do that. He will not change the Constitution in order to benefit himself.'[6]

I happened to meet Mandela shortly afterwards and asked him what led to his utterance. He told me he had met a group of British politicians who expressed precisely that concern – and that the matter be dealt with 'while I am still alive', he chuckled.

There was an echo here of previous utterances by Mandela on the subject.

So, shortly before the launch of our election campaign, I directly addressed the issue in Durban: 'Mandela has already seen fit to declare that Mbeki would never do such a thing [seek a third term] but our president himself has refused to answer. We need to clear the decks on this critical issue ...'

There was a fluttering in the dovecotes. I was accused by Mbeki's spokesman of 'electioneering' (actually, it *was* an election). But since so much of the presidency was shrouded in secrecy, I could hardly expect anything unequivocal, least of all concerning Mbeki's political calculations.

But, once the issue achieved critical media mass, a denial eventually emerged. One of Mbeki's chief admirers in the media, editor Mathatha Tsedu, denounced me as 'a racist'. Even raising the question, he ventured, 'is a great insult to many black citizens'.[7]

Tsedu's predictable – and thought-blocking – response did not prevent me from adding that, even if Mbeki did not crassly move to amend the constitution, he might seek the 'Lurleen option'. This referred to the name of the wife of one-time term-limited Alabama governor, George Wallace, who simply ran his cancer-stricken wife as governor and landed up back in power as a consequence. I suggested Mbeki might wish to continue as party president and have a surrogate elected to the official post.

Events, as the ANC succession struggle unfolded three years later, pointed exactly in that direction.

Indeed the ruling party's triumph at the polls in 2004 masked the increasing resentment in its restive ranks against the centralising and ever more authoritarian impulses of Mbeki. When he discharged Zuma from the deputy presidency in June 2005 – for complicity revealed in a corruption trial – he would in fact detonate an explosion of such thermonuclear intensity that he would have his own presidency eviscerated when, in 2008, the party removed him as head of state.

And, as I had warned, he did attempt to extend his own term as party president at the ANC conference in 2007. What I had not envisaged in my initial warning was that he would be resoundingly defeated by Jacob Zuma, the very man who Mandela had told me years before was the 'key man' in the party. Within months, Zuma would – improbably – become the next president of South Africa.

CHAPTER TWENTY-ONE

Finale

I N DECEMBER 2004, I had my last face-to-face encounter with Mandela, this time at his Bishopscourt home in Cape Town. There was no agenda on either side – it was simply a courtesy call, with my wife and a young parliamentary colleague anxious to capture a 'Kodak moment' for posterity.

By this stage his physical frailties were far more apparent than ever: he could not rise from his chair and remained seated for the duration of our conversation and photo sessions. But the discussion flowed along its normal agreeable lines. He was particularly scornful of US President George W Bush and his decision the year before to invade Iraq, where a full-scale insurrection was still in progress at the time of our get-together.

Indeed, this matter had fully engaged Mandela's attention and outspokenness for some time. When America had decided to bypass UN processes to mount its attack, Mandela had declared that the US president's contempt for the UN lay in the fact that its secretary general, Kofi Annan, was black.[1]

I asked Mandela whether he really believed that Bush, who, for all his false steps in governance, had appointed both the first African-American secretary of state (Colin Powell) and national security advisor (Condoleezza Rice) could really be described as 'racist'. He was adamant on the point; I thought better than to point out to him the stinging put-down that his remark elicited from left-wing polemicist Christopher Hitchens, otherwise an admirer of Mandela, who had noted: 'It's a strong field in which to compete, but the contest for the most stupid remark about the confrontation with Saddam Hussein has apparently been won by Nelson Mandela'.[2]

This then led into a discussion of various American presidents. Mandela indicated that he had considerable regard for the elder Bush (George HW Bush) and, of course, for Bill Clinton, a firm friend of his. As it happened, I was then reading an admiring but very revealing biography of Ronald Reagan by his speech-writer – Peggy Noonan.[3] I told Mandela that it was interesting to read how Reagan's political and economic philosophy, so different from his own, had arisen in the midst of an extremely impoverished childhood, beset by an alcoholic father and early setbacks that helped forge both his character and his determination to succeed.

Mandela indicated that he, too, found Reagan to be a fascinating character and had hoped, on his first visit to the United States after his release from prison, to meet with him. 'But,' Mandela wistfully observed, 'he was one of the very few people who refused to meet with me.' I was very surprised at this snub, notwithstanding Reagan's staunch opposition both to the ANC and to the isolation of apartheid South Africa.

When, some three years later, then a resident at Harvard University, I recounted this story to Ken Duberstein, who had served as Reagan's chief of staff and was a director of the Institute of Politics where I was a fellow, he doubted its veracity. 'Reagan was the politest of people. It is inconceivable that he would ever have refused Mandela in that way,' he said.

As our conversation drew to its conclusion, Michal and I noticed that Mandela repeated to us a story he had told us when we first arrived.

But during our last conversation – this time by telephone – some two years later, there was no apparent fog in his memory. I had just announced that, after thirteen rather eventful years at the helm, I would soon stand down as leader of my party.[4] Some days after the announcement, in early December 2006, I received a call from Mandela, from Mozambique. It was vintage Madiba. He bantered about 'giving me such a shock at my vast age with your decision'. And then, in more serious tone, he said: 'You know, Tony, you will be missed much more than you might realise, because you have played such a very important role in our country … much more than you will ever read about.'

What a grace note, I thought, to mark the end of a relationship, which, I suddenly realised on that day, now stretched back more than fourteen years to a time when the prospects of planting a democracy on the stony soil of South Africa seemed far from assured.

Mandela had retired from the presidency in 1999, at the height of his popularity and acclaim at home and abroad. When he left office, South Africa stood high in international acclaim and in the indices that matter in the world. He remained, until his last formal appearance at the opening match of the FIFA Football World Cup in South Africa in June 2010 – which his famous persona had done much to secure – a constant presence in the affairs of his country and the wider world.

Great age and greater infirmity marked the years that followed, until his death, at the age of ninety-five, on 5 December 2013. He was mourned throughout the land and across the globe, as the world bowed its head at the passing of greatness. In barrels of ink and gridfuls of electrons, obeisance was paid to his remarkable leadership. One tribute, I thought, captured the essence of his inspirational example. 'He was neither a genius nor, as he often said himself, a saint …', *The Economist* editorialised. His 'shortcomings … pale into insignificance when set against the magnitude of his overall achievement. It is hard to think of anyone else in the world in recent times with whom every single person, in every corner of the Earth, can somehow identify. He was, quite simply, a wonderful man.'[5]

The years between his relinquishing office and his death were marked by tumult at home and abroad: the global financial crisis of 2007–2008 had tilted the balance of the world economy, although there were no apparent winners and an ever greater circle of losers, from southern Europe to the United States and even mighty China, whose roaring economy was starting to slow. Nations and commodities fell in and out of favour, and in again and out again, with nervous and ever more fickle investor sentiment. South Africa was hit hard as its currency cratered, a reflection of its widening twin (trade and fiscal) deficits, oscillating global sentiment on emerging market economies and multiple own goals at home.

When Mandela left the presidency in 1999 the currency, the rand, traded against the US dollar in the R6.00 range; when he died in December 2013 it had fallen to around R10.69, a decline of over 40 per cent, on a measurement sometimes indicated as the 'sovereign's share price'. In 1998/1999, the country ranked top in Africa, at forty-seventh place, on the World Economic Forum's global competitiveness index of 148 nations; by 2013/2014 it had fallen six positions to fifty-third, now second in Africa to Mauritius.[6]

Far more precipitous – and explicable by the cascading corruption drenching the state – was South Africa's slide down the rankings in perceptions of corruption. When Mandela left office, his country was rated thirty-fourth on Transparency International's index.[7] By the time of his death in 2013, it had fallen to seventy-second place out of 177 nations surveyed.[8]

Mandela's presidency made little impact on the country's serious and structural unemployment crisis, a key and continuing failure of governance, and today the position has worsened, with fewer than two in five working-age adults having jobs in formal employment.[9]

The many blunders of the presidents (Mbeki and Zuma) who followed Mandela have been well chronicled, and, in the case of the latter, his first term of office had yet to be completed at the time of this writing.

But of the welter of difficulties challenging Zuma – both inherited and self-inflicted – one of the lesser stumbles during his tenure, this one in the quicksand of culture, drew a sharp distinction between him and Mandela.

In May 2012, a Johannesburg art gallery displayed a satirical painting, 'The Spear', by local artist Brett Murray of Jacob Zuma in Lenin-like pose, but with his genitalia exposed. Doubtless the president's brushes with sexual scandal, his sexual indiscretions revealed during his rape trial, his fathering many illegitimate children and his polygamous lifestyle, inspired the work.[10] The reaction from Zuma's attorneys and the ruling power, as well as those in its orbit, was fast and furious. Law suits, street marches on the gallery and the defacement of the painting were among the responses. The ANC went so far as to call for its members to boycott a major weekly newspaper *City Press* for displaying the work on its website. Its editor buckled under the pressure and censored her own website.

Mandela, who indeed had a keen sense of humour, including the ability to laugh at himself, had his own 'Spear' moment, though how he defused it was very telling. He had an aversion to censoring anything, even pornography. In February 1998, *Hustler* magazine indecorously named Mandela its 'Asshole of the Month'. Then deputy minister of Home Affairs, Lindiwe Sisulu, slammed the issue as 'vile, outrageous and obscene', and apparently considered banning it. Mandela, in sharp contrast, 'laughed the matter off' and, instead of rushing to court, he said, somewhat oxymoronically, that the magazine 'should use its own sense of morality and judgement'. He surprised his director general, Jakes Gerwel, by asking impishly: 'Have you seen this month's *Hustler*?'[11]

More consequentially, it was Mandela's attitude towards the courts and his faith in the supremacy of the constitution and respect for its institutions that separated him from his successors.

Indeed, President Jacob Zuma's own ascent to office can be, diplomatically, best described as a Houdini-like escape from the coils of court procedures and the multiple corruption charges he avoided before becoming president, rather than an acceptance of them. In contrast to Mandela's high regard for the constitution, which he both championed and signed into law, the recent scepticism of senior ANC national executive member and Deputy Minister of Correctional Services Ngoako Ramatlhodi, provides a studied contrast. In 2011, he stated that the constitutional transition was a victory for 'apartheid forces' who wanted to 'retain white domination under a black government'. This was achieved 'by emptying the legislature and executive of real power' and giving it to 'the other constitutional institutions and civil society movements'.[12] Apparently, other powerful voices in Mr Ramatlhodi's party and government share this sentiment.

We might conclude from this contrast that, while the ruling party embraces Nelson Mandela and his early legacy of struggle, revolution and sacrifice, it is far more ambivalent about what I have termed 'latter Mandelaism', such as his respect for the restraints on unfettered state power, and many of the presidential characteristics I have enumerated in this book.

In January 2014, less than a month after Mandela's burial, another controversy over his real legacy arose. Professor Stephen Ellis, a professor of social sciences in the Netherlands, had previously published a groundbreaking book on the ANC in exile, entitled *External Mission*.[13] That work lifted the veils of secrecy of the decades when many in the movement's top leadership lived abroad. It provided a harsh and meticulously researched account of the secrecy, shenanigans and factionalised – even murderous – 'struggles within the struggle'. On finishing reading it, I was left with the conclusion that, perhaps, one advantage for Mandela of his prison years was that he had been spared being touched by some of these ANC exile networks, which, according to Ellis, were heavily involved in corruption and criminality and even colluded with elements of the apartheid security police.

Now the author turned his attention, spurred by a lengthy transcript of Mandela's draft political biography, which he had secretly handwritten in jail and which had recently come to light, to a sharp difference between this text and his somewhat more sanitised bestselling autobiography, *Long Walk to Freedom*,[14] which had been published in 1994, the year his presidency began.

According to Ellis, the biggest difference between the two texts was 'the abundance of information in the prison memoir on Mandela's personal relationship with the SACP [South African Communist Party] and his embrace of the main tenets of Marxism-Leninism.'[15]

While the author concedes on the basis of the text that there was no evidence that Mandela ever formally joined the SACP (although in other works he suggested that he had at some stage been a member), he provides extracts from the prison draft that showed, among other things, Mandela's 'intensity of attachment to Marxism by the late 1950s if not earlier' and his admiration for Soviet foreign policy. Ellis drily notes that such passages were 'not included in *Long Walk to Freedom*'.

While I thought this matter of some historic interest, I was far less certain of its enduring significance. Indeed, some months before Ellis's article, and in the last stages of Mandela's life, a lively debate had raged in the correspondence section of the *New York Review of Books* about how Mandela's attachment to Communism had shaped his views and conduct. Bill Keller, who had served as Johannesburg bureau chief for the *New York Times* at the stage when Mandela was released from prison, provided, I thought, the correct perspective on both Mandela's enduring values and his powers of adaptiveness, or political flexibility. In response to a charge that Keller had elided the close connection between Mandela and the Communists, he wrote:

Nelson Mandela was, at various times, a black nationalist and a non-racialist, an opponent of armed struggle and a practitioner of armed struggle, a close partner of the South African Communist Party and, in his presidency, a close partner of South Africa's powerful capitalists. In other words, he was whatever served his purpose of ending South Africa's fiendish brand of minority rule. I should not have been so categorical in saying that Mandela was not a Communist. But he was not a Communist in the values he upheld, the politics he practiced, the constitution he negotiated, or the presidency he held.[16]

But let me conclude with a note of hope about how the spirit of democracy, freedom and robust dialogue has actually taken root a decade and a half since Mandela left formal office and entered the 'twilight of greatness' before his death.

During his presidency, South Africa's parliamentary opposition was deeply fragmented, its civil society was still finding its feet after the long dark night of apartheid, and the press, whose leading editors were mostly drawn from the minority, was at some quite decisive moments, mute and offside. The radiance of Mandela's leadership, ironically, both warmed our hearts but also sometimes blinded 'some among us' (to borrow a favourite phrase of former President Mbeki) to our roles and the rules of engagement needed for democratic deepening.

In this respect, at least, there has been a sea change today. Without the protection of what *The Economist* dubbed 'Mandela's saintly aura',[17] both the ruling party and its leaders will be more harshly judged. Difficult for them, perhaps, but positive for the country's long-term democratic prospects. This was apparent during the official memorial service for

Mandela at the FNB Stadium in Soweto. In a moment, or several of them, of exquisite embarrassment, President Jacob Zuma was roundly booed by sections of the large audience in front of more than ninety world leaders and millions watching on television.

Days after Mandela's funeral near his birthplace in Qunu in the Eastern Cape, the powerful National Union of Metalworkers of South Africa (NUMSA) trade union announced it was disaffiliating from the ruling ANC, whose factiousness was starting to resemble a circular firing squad. Doubtless it will still remain in power for some years yet, but the Madiba aura appears to be non-transferrable to his political heirs, and thus normality begins to settle on the country's politics.

Earlier in the same momentous year, in June 2013, Constitutional Court Justice Edwin Cameron delivered an influential address at the Sunday Times Literary Awards. He eloquently described how, in one vital respect, and despite the considerable damage done, the country's democracy remains afloat:

> Our polity is boisterous, rowdy, sometimes cacophonous and often angry. That much is to be expected. But after nearly two decades, we have far more freedom, more debate, more robust and direct engagement with each other – and certainly more practically tangible social justice than 20 years ago.[18]

The push-back by a diverse range of civil society actors and the delayed passage and marked improvement to the Protection of State Information Bill in the year of Mandela's death was a striking, encouraging example.

Just four years before Nelson Mandela's 1990 release and his walk back into freedom, another famous political prisoner was released from jail, the first in the Soviet Union to be freed by Mikhail Gorbachev. Natan Sharansky had also been convicted and imprisoned for high treason. After nine years in jail, he went into exile in Israel and subsequently became a political leader there. In 2004, he published a powerful polemic, *The Case for Democracy*, in which he elaborates, with passion and clarity, the idea that freedom is rooted in the right to dissent, to walk into the town square and declare one's views without fear of consequence.[19]

For the many things that have gone right and wrong with South Africa since our first steps under Mandela's leadership towards becoming a free society back in 1994, Sharansky's universal observation that 'the democracy which sometimes dislikes us is a much safer place than the dictatorship which loves us' must serve both as guide and as inspiration into the future.

Mandela was, in so many ways, a once-in-a-nation's-lifetime offer. After his death, another South African Nobel laureate, novelist JM Coetzee, wrote: 'He was, and by the time of his death was universally held to be, a great man; he may well be the last of the great men, as the concept of greatness retires into the historical shadows.'[20]

But we should look upon him and learn from him, even if we do not ever see his like again.

ENDNOTES

INTRODUCTION

1 Tony Leon, *On the Contrary – Leading the Opposition in a Democratic South Africa*, p498.
2 Richard Stengel, *Mandela's Way – Lessons on Life, Love, and Courage*, pp5–7.
3 Ibid.
4 Z Pallo Jordan, 'Big Brother Would Turn Luxuriant Green with Envy', *Business Day Live*, 1 August 2013.
5 Richard Stengel, *Mandela's Way*, p4.
6 Stanley Greenberg, *Dispatches from the War Room – In the Trenches with Five Extraordinary Leaders*, p15.
7 Anthony Sampson, *Mandela – The Authorised Biography*, p532.
8 'Politics the Victim of Vavi Debacle', *Financial Mail*, 2–7 August 2013.
9 Nelson Mandela, 'Nelson Mandela's Address to the International Press Institute Congress', 14 February 1994, http://www.anc.org.za/show.php?id=3651.
10 During my tenure at the helm, the Democratic Party (DP) changed its name to the Democratic Alliance (DA).

CHAPTER ONE

1 Tony Leon, *On the Contrary*, p180.
2 Ibid., pp180–181.
3 Alec Russell, 'White Man Unburdened', *Financial Times*, 23–24 January 2010.
4 Ibid.
5 Anthony Sampson, *Mandela*, p403.
6 Ibid., p407.
7 Michael Morris, 'How Can We Still Realise Madiba's Hopes, Dreams?', *Cape Argus*, 11 February 2010.
8 Martin Meredith, *Mandela – A Biography*, p401.
9 Stephen Watson, 'Voting with my Feet', in *The Music in the Ice, On Writers, Writing & Other Things*, p318.
10 Martin Meredith, *Mandela*, p403.
11 Patti Waldmeir, *Anatomy of a Miracle*, p241.

12 Tony Leon, *On the Contrary*, especially chapter 5 'Present at the Creation', pp177–234.
13 Patti Waldmeir, *Anatomy of a Miracle*, p206.

CHAPTER TWO

1 Joe Slovo, 'Has Socialism Failed?', 1989, http://www.marxists.org/subject/africa/slovo/1989/socialism-failed.htm.
2 Mandela had been an attorney in Johannesburg in the 1950s, when my father was a junior advocate at the Bar.

CHAPTER THREE

1 Quoted by Hermann Giliomee in Milton Shain's *Opposing Voices*, p69.
2 Patti Waldmeir, *Anatomy of a Miracle*, p193.

CHAPTER FOUR

1 Patti Waldmeir, *Anatomy of a Miracle*, pp191–192.
2 Ibid., p192.
3 Martin Meredith, *Mandela*, p413.
4 See, for example, Tony Leon, *On the Contrary*, pp183–232; Patti Waldmeir, *Anatomy of a Miracle*, pp190–250; Martin Meredith, *Mandela*, pp439–480; and Anthony Sampson, *Mandela*, pp422–456.
5 Martin Meredith, *Mandela*, p441.
6 *New York Review of Books*, 21 December 2006, p38.
7 The legal advocates' Bar.

CHAPTER FIVE

1 Patti Waldmeir, *Anatomy of a Miracle*, p203.
2 Sources diverge about the exact date, but it is likely to have been on 25 or 26 June.
3 Patti Waldmeir, *Anatomy of a Miracle*, p203.
4 Anthony Sampson, *Mandela*, pp464–465.
5 Ibid., p468.
6 Ibid., p469.

CHAPTER SIX

1 *Nelson Mandela: From Freedom to the Future – Tributes and Speeches*, pp148–149.
2 In other words, he was not a certifiable member of Zulu royalty through the patriarchal line.

CHAPTER SEVEN

1 The Robben Island prison.
2 A predecessor of the Democratic Party.

3 'ANC Man Who Ordered Shell House Shooting Ensured Election', SA Press Association (SAPA), 10 May 1998.
4 Anthony Sampson, *Mandela*, p485.
5 Martin Meredith, *Mandela*, p508.
6 Ibid., p509.
7 Ibid.
8 *Hansard*, National Assembly, Interpellations, Vol 3, 1994, p11.
9 Ibid.
10 Ibid.
11 *Cape Times*, 2 June 1995.

CHAPTER EIGHT
1 FW de Klerk, *The Last Trek – A New Beginning*, p354.
2 Ibid. p347.
3 Ibid. p362.
4 Anthony Sampson, *Mandela*, p511.
5 FW de Klerk, *The Last Trek*, p349.
6 Ibid.
7 Ibid.
8 Ibid., p352.
9 Ibid.

CHAPTER NINE
1 Buthelezi said Sifiso drew the gun, but Sifiso and SABC chief executive Zwelakhe Sisulu claimed it was one of Buthelezi's bodyguards.
2 'Buthelezi Storms Television Studio', *Associated Press*, 26 September 1994.
3 Mandela's remarks, as quoted to Parliament by MG Buthelezi MP, *Hansard*, 2 May 1995, cols 716–722.
4 *Hansard*, 2 May 1995, col 719.
5 *Hansard*, 2 May 1995, cols 819–820.
6 As quoted by Jack Bloom MPL in 'The Case for George W Bush', address to SA Institute for International Affairs, Johannesburg, 5 September 2006.
7 Ibid.

CHAPTER TEN
1 Anthony Sampson, *Mandela*, p506.
2 'Davis–Pityana Row Cools to a Simmer', *Mail & Guardian*, 22 March 1996.
3 Ibid.
4 Ibid.
5 'Do We Want Quality or Ethnic Cleansing', *Mail & Guardian*, 22 December 1995.

CHAPTER ELEVEN

1 *The Sowetan,* 31 January 1997.
2 *Cape Times,* 24 January 1997.
3 *The Mercury,* 24 January 1997.
4 *Volksblad,* 10 January 1997.
5 *The Citizen,* 30 January 1997.
6 Personal records.
7 *Cape Times,* 27 February 1997.
8 *Die Burger,* 4 March 1997.
9 *Pretoria News,* 7 March 1997.

CHAPTER TWELVE

1 www.aryan-nation.org/Wake_Up_or_Die.pdf.
2 Martin Meredith, *Mandela,* p524.
3 Anthony Sampson, *Mandela,* p523.
4 Cyril Ramaphosa, 'Whites Don't Understand What Blacks Mean by "the Boers"',
   Politcsweb, 15 November 2013.
5 Martin Meredith, *Mandela,* p523.
6 A good and reasonably dispassionate account of the TRC's *modus operandi* and
   reactions to it appears in Martin Meredith's work *The State of Africa – A History of Fifty
   Years of Independence* (published in the US as *The Fate of Africa*), pp654 onwards.
7 Martin Meredith, *The State of Africa,* p657.
8 Ibid.
9 Ibid., p659.
10 Allister Sparks, *Beyond the Miracle – Inside the New South Africa,* p161.
11 Martin Meredith, *The State of Africa,* p656.

CHAPTER THIRTEEN

1 Nelson Mandela, 'South Africa's Future Foreign Policy', *Foreign Affairs,* 1 December
   1993.
2 'For Sale SA's Diplomatic Relations', *Mail & Guardian,* 8 December 1995.
3 Marilyn Berger, 'Suharto Dies at 86; Indonesian Dictator Brought Order and
   Bloodshed', *New York Times,* 28 January 2008.
4 Stefaans Brummer, 'Mandela's Strange Links to Human Rights Abuser', *Mail &
   Guardian,* 26 May 1995.
5 Tom Lodge: 'Nelson Mandela: Assessing the Icon', *Open Democracy,* 18 July 2008.
6 See, for example, *Hansard,* 4 June 1997, cols 1331–1334; and *Hansard,* 5 November
   1997, cols 3483–3484.
7 SA Press Association (SAPA), 6 June 1995.
8 Anthony Sampson, *Mandela,* p558.

CHAPTER FOURTEEN

1 Martin Meredith, *Mandela*, p519.
2 Ibid., p.520
3 David Beresford, 'Nelson Mandela Obituary – Hero of the apartheid struggle, he spent 26 years in jail and became South Africa's first democratically elected president', *The Guardian*, 5 December 2013.
4 Ibid.
5 Anthony Sampson, *Mandela*, p518.
6 'Mandela's Long Walk is Not Yet Over', *Financial Times*, 6 December 2013.
7 Clayton Swart, 'Billions Flowed into South Africa Thanks to Mandela', *Business Day*, 9 December 2013.
8 http://www.oecd.org/industry/inv/investmentstatisticsandanalysis/2422913.pdf. According to South Africa's official export and foreign direct investment promotion agency, Trade and Investment South Africa, investment flows grew from R1 348 000 000 in 1994 to some R9 184 000 000 by 1999.
9 http://www.indexmundi.com/facts/south-africa/foreign-direct-investment. Despite sharp fluctuations, the following figures from the International Monetary Fund's Balance of Payments Statistics Yearbook and data files show the significant FDI gains, in dollar terms, in the course of Mandela's presidency: 1994: $374 410 400; 1995: $1 248 425 000; 1996: $816 389 200; 1997: $3 810 544 000; 1998: $550 338 600; and 1999: $1 503 332 000.
10 http://www.eisa.org.za/WEP/souoverview8.htm. While economic growth rose from 1.2% in 1993 to 3.2% in 1994, and held to a mean of 3.6% until 1996, it fell sharply in 1997 and remained at a low 1.8% until 1999 – this despite projected growth of 6% a year required to meet GEAR's job creation targets.

CHAPTER FIFTEEN

1 Tony Leon, *On the Contrary*, p320.
2 She claimed they were from a European Union (EU) grant, although the EU ambassadors then invited me to a lunch and advised that, if such was the case, the funds had not been authorised for this purpose.
3 Martin Meredith, *Mandela*, p546.
4 Ibid.
5 'Sacked Holomisa Accuses Mbeki of Collusion', SA Press Association (SAPA), 1 August 1996.
6 Anthony Sampson, *Mandela*, p538.

CHAPTER SIXTEEN

1 Anthony Sampson, *Mandela*, p579.
2 Ibid., p517.
3 'Media on the Menu', *Rhodes Journalism Review*, December 1996, p7.
4 Tony Leon, *On the Contrary*, p478.
5 The successor to the United Democratic Front (UDF).

6 Jean-Paul Sartre wrote an introduction to Frantz Fanon's *Les Damnés de la Terre* (*The Wretched of the Earth*), which deals with the dehumanising effects of colonialism.
7 See in particular, John Carlin, *The Independent,* London, 21 September 1990 and 14 May 1991.
8 Emma Gilbey, *The Lady – The Life and Times of Winnie Mandela.*
9 Truth and Reconciliation Commission of South Africa Report, Special Investigation: Mandela United Football Club, 1998, Vol 2, Chapter 6, pp565–579 para 104.
10 *Hansard,* 9 August 1994, cols 1010–1017.
11 Ibid.
12 *Hansard,* 26 August 1994, cols 2099–2105.
13 Ibid.
14 Ibid.
15 *Weekend Argus,* 27–28 August 1994.
16 A full account of my tangles with Mrs Madikizela-Mandela, and significant additional background material, appears in Chapter 13 of *On the Contrary,* pp471–491.

CHAPTER SEVENTEEN

1 *Hurley v Minister of Law and Order and Another* 1985 (4) SA 709 (D). For comment on this case, see *South African Law Journal,* Vol 103, 1986, p344; Professor LJ Boulle in *South African Journal on Human Rights,* Vol 1, 1985, pp251–260; and John Hlophe in *South African Law Journal,* Vol 104, 1987, p183.
2 Maiden speech of ME Mbili MP, 17 October 2006, *Hansard,* unrevised. Mr Mbili served in parliament for six years, until he was killed in a motorcar accident in July 2012.
3 *Hansard,* 25 February 1999, col 81.
4 The premier referred the findings of the commission to the attorney general who in January 1999 cleared her of corruption and fraud charges after she agreed to pay back all amounts owing by her to her former department in an amount of R27 000.
5 See, 'Outcry over Disgraced Duarte's Top Job', *IOL News,* 19 August 1999; and SA Press Association (SAPA), 12 February 1998.
6 *S v Zondo,* Natal Provincial Division (NPD), April 1986 (unreported).
7 Ibid.
8 The Leon Commission Report compiled in 1994 led to the rewriting of South Africa's mining health and safety legislation via Act 29 of 1996 (Mine Health and Safety Act).

CHAPTER EIGHTEEN

1 Mike Nicol, *Mandela – The Authorised Portrait,* p290.
2 SA Press Association (SAPA), 1 March 1996.
3 *Cape Times,* 4 March 1996.
4 James Myburgh, *The Last Jacobins of Africa – Thabo Mbeki and the Making of the New South Africa,* unpublished manuscript, 2007, p95, quoting an unnamed ANC official reported in the *Chicago Tribune.*

5 http://www.sahistory.org.za/archive/report-president-anc-nelson-mandela-50th-national-conference-african-national-congress-mafik.

6 Ibid.

7 Ibid.

8 Anthony Sampson, *Mandela*, p542.

9 James Myburgh, *The Last Jacobins of Africa*, p97.

10 The document is contained in *Umrabulo* No 5, Third Quarter 1998, as quoted by Myburgh, p117.

11 *Hansard*, 10 February 1998, cols 39–57.

12 'The Death of the Rainbow Nation: Unmasking the ANC's Programme for Re-racialisation', Democratic Party discussion document, February 1998.

13 *Business Day*, 5 March 1998.

14 *Business Day*, 8 March 1998.

15 Anthony Sampson, *Mandela*, pp576–577.

16 Ibid.

CHAPTER NINETEEN

1 Interview on Radio 702, Johannesburg, 6 December 2013.

2 *Hansard*, 26 March 1999, cols 194–196.

3 Ibid.

CHAPTER TWENTY

1 Quoted by RW Johnson in *South Africa's Brave New World – The Beloved Country Since the End of Apartheid*, p135. The author asserts that this speech appeared in print for the first time in 2006. Mandela's authorised biographer, Anthony Sampson, provides a more benign explanation, stating that it was delivered at the end of the conference 'when many of the media had left' (Sampson, *Mandela*, p543).

2 Martin Meredith, *Mandela*, p585. Curiously, in the Afterword to the authorised biography by Anthony Sampson (*Mandela*) (written by John Battersby, pp587–611), which covers this period, this spat is not mentioned.

3 Parliament, 21 October 2004 (online text), www.anc.org.za/docs/anctoday/2004/at42.htm.

4 'Mbeki Loses the Plot', *The Economist*, 3 May 2001.

5 Iraq Profile, BBC News Middle East, http://www.bbc.co.uk/news/world-middle-east-14546763.

6 *The Citizen*, 29 July 2003.

7 *City Press*, 15 February 2004.

CHAPTER TWENTY-ONE

1 www.iol.co.za, 30 January 2003.

2 Christopher Hitchens, 'Race and Rescue – Nelson Mandela's Odious Views on Iraq',

Slate, 1 February 2003.

3 Peggy Noonan, *When Character was King: A Story of Ronald Reagan,* Penguin Books, 2002.

4 My decision to resign as leader of the Democratic Alliance and leader of the official opposition in parliament was announced on 26 November 2006 and became effective on 6 May 2007.

5 'A Giant Passes', *The Economist,* 5 December 2013.

6 'How the world rates South Africa', http://www.southafrica.info/business/economy/globalsurveys.htm#competitiveness.

7 http://archive.transparency.org/policy_research/surveys_indices/cpi/previous_cpi/1999.

8 http://www.transparency.org/cpi2013/results#myAnchor11.

9 'A Giant Passes', *The Economist.*

10 See, for example, Wikipedia, the free encyclopaedia, http://en.wikipedia.org/wiki/The_Spear_(painting).

11 Anthony Sampson, *Mandela,* p528.

12 Justice Edwin Cameron, 'Constitution Holding Steady in the Storm', *Sunday Times,* 30 June 2013.

13 Stephen Ellis, *External Mission – The ANC in Exile.*

14 Nelson Mandela, *Long Walk to Freedom.*

15 Stephen Ellis, 'New Light on Nelson Mandela's Autobiography', *Politicsweb,* 13 January 2014.

16 'Mandela & Communism, An Exchange', *New York Review of Books,* 6 June 2013.

17 'A Giant Passes', *The Economist.*

18 Justice Edwin Cameron, 'Constitution Holding Steady in the Storm'.

19 Natan Sharansky, *The Case for Democracy – The Power of Freedom to Overcome Tyranny & Terror,* pp41–42.

20 JM Coetzee: 'On Nelson Mandela (1918–2013)', *The New York Review of Books,* 9 January–5 February 2014, p8.

'A Giant Passes' (2013) *The Economist,* 5 December, http://www.economist.com/blogs/baobab/2013/12/nelson-mandela-0.

'ANC Man Who Ordered Shell House Shooting Ensured Election' (1998) SA Press Association (SAPA), 10 May.

Asmal, Kader, Chidester, David and James, Wilmot G (eds.) (2003) *Nelson Mandela: From Freedom to the Future – Speeches and Tributes.* Johannesburg: Jonathan Ball.

Beresford, David (2013) 'Nelson Mandela Obituary – Hero of the apartheid struggle, he spent 26 years in jail and became South Africa's first democratically elected president', *The Guardian,* 5 December, http://www.theguardian.com/world/2013/dec/05/nelson-mandela-obituary.

Berger, Marilyn (2008) 'Suharto Dies at 86; Indonesian Dictator Brought Order and Bloodshed', *New York Times,* 28 January, http://www.nytimes.com/2008/01/28/world/asia/28suharto.html?pagewanted=all&_r=0.

Brummer, Stefaans (1995) 'Mandela's Strange Links to Human Rights Abuser', *Mail & Guardian,* 26 May, http://mg.co.za/article/1995-05-26-mandelas-strange-links-to-human-rights-abuser.

'Buthelezi Storms Television Studio' (1994) *Associated Press Archive,* 26 September, http://www.apnewsarchive.com/1994/Buthelezi-Storms-Television-Studio-Legal-Action-Threatened/id-55a15699bfd46fc27264693a034dcc87.

Cameron, Edwin (2013) 'Constitution Holding Steady in the Storm', *Sunday Times,* 30 June.

Carlin, John (2013) *Knowing Mandela.* London: Atlantic Books.

Coetzee, JM (2014) 'On Nelson Mandela (1918–2013)' *The New York Review of Books,* 9 January–5 February, http://www.nybooks.com/articles/archives/2014/jan/09/nelson-mandela-1918-2013/.

'Davis–Pityana Row Cools to a Simmer' (1996) *Mail & Guardian,* 22 March, http://mg.co.za/article/1996-03-22-davis-pityana-row-cools-to-a-simmer.

De Klerk, FW (1998) *The Last Trek – A New Beginning.* Basingstoke: Pan Macmillan.

'Do We Want Quality or Ethnic Cleansing' (1995) *Mail & Guardian,* 22 December, http://mg.co.za/article/1995-12-22-do-we-want-quality-or-ethnic-cleansing.

Ellis, Stephen (2012) *External Mission – The ANC in Exile.* Johannesburg: Jonathan Ball.

Ellis, Stephen (2014) 'New Light on Nelson Mandela's Autobiography'. *Politicsweb,* 13 January, http://politicsweb.co.za/politicsweb/view/politicsweb/en/page71654?oid=509092&sn=Detail&pid=71654.

BIBLIOGRAPHY

'For Sale SA's Diplomatic Relations' (1995) *Mail & Guardian*, 8 December, http://mg.co. za/article/1995-12-08-for-sale-sas-diplomatic-relations.

Gilbey, Emma (1993) *The Lady – The Life and Times of Winnie Mandela*. London: Jonathan Cape.

Greenberg, Stanley (2009) *Dispatches from the War Room – In the Trenches with Five Extraordinary Leaders*. New York: Thomas Dunne Books.

Hitchens, Christopher (2003) 'Race and Rescue – Nelson Mandela's Odious Views on Iraq', *Slate*, 1 February, http://www.slate.com/articles/news_and_politics/fighting_words/2003/02/race_and_rescue.html.

Johnson, RW (2009) *South Africa's Brave New World – The Beloved Country Since the End of Apartheid*. London: Allen Lane.

Jordan, Z Pallo (2013) 'Big Brother Would Turn Luxuriant Green with Envy', *Business Day Live*, 1 August, www.bdlive.co.za/opinion/columnists/2013/08/01/big-brother-would-turnluxuriant-green-with-envy.

Leon, Tony (2008) *On the Contrary – Leading the Opposition in a Democratic South Africa*. Johannesburg: Jonathan Ball.

Lodge, Tom (2008) 'Nelson Mandela: Assessing the Icon', *Open Democracy*, 18 July, http://www.opendemocracy.net/article/democracy_power/africa/nelson-mandela-at-90.

'Mandela & Communism: An Exchange' (2013) *New York Review of Books*, 6 June, http://www.nybooks.com/articles/archives/2013/jun/06/mandela-communism-exchange/.

Mandela, Nelson (1993) 'South Africa's Future Foreign Policy', *Foreign Affairs*, 1 December (web 25 November 2013), http://www.foreignaffairs.com/articles/49408/nelson-mandela/south-africas-future-foreign-policy.

Mandela, Nelson (1994) *Long Walk to Freedom*. New York: Little Brown.

Mandela, Nelson (1994) 'Nelson Mandela's Address to the International Press Institute Congress', 14 February, http://www.anc.org.za/show.php?id=3651.

Mandela, Nelson (2010) *Conversations with Myself*. London: Macmillan.

'Mandela's Long Walk is Not Yet Over' (2013) *Financial Times*, 6 December, http://www.ft.com/cms/s/0/c3a7be34-5e81-11e3-a44c-00144feabdco.html#axzz2rmwbpwmf.

'Mbeki Loses the Plot' (2001) *The Economist*, 3 May, http://www.economist.com/node/613284.

'Media on the Menu' (1996) *Rhodes Journalism Review*, Grahamstown, December, http://www.rjr.ru.ac.za/rjrpdf/rjr_no13/rjr_no13.pdf.

Meredith, Martin (2010) *Mandela – A Biography*. Johannesburg: Simon & Schuster/Jonathan Ball.

Meredith Martin (2005) *The State of Africa – A History of Fifty Years of Independence*. Johannesburg: Jonathan Ball.

Morris, Michael (2010) 'How Can We Still Realise Madiba's Hopes, Dreams?', *Cape Argus*, 11 February,

Myburgh, James (2007) *The Last Jacobins of Africa – Thabo Mbeki and the Making of the New South Africa*. Unpublished manuscript.

New York Review of Books (2006) 21 December, http://www.nybooks.com/articles/archives/2006/dec/21/the-enigma-of-ariel-sharon/

Nicol, Mike (2006) *Mandela – The Authorised Portrait*. Auckland: PQ Blackwell.

'Outcry over Disgraced Duarte's Top Job' (1999) *IOL News*, 19 August, http://www.iol.co.za/news/politics/outcry-over-disgraced-duarte-s-top-job-1.9521#.UuoLvmQW2Io.

'Politics the Victim of Vavi Debacle' (2013) *Financial Mail*, 2–7 August.

Ramaphosa, Cyril (2013) 'Whites Don't Understand What Blacks Mean by "the Boers"', *Politcsweb*, 15 November, http://www.politicsweb.co.za/politicsweb/view/politicsweb/en/page71654?oid=455815&sn=Detail&pid=71616.

Russell, Alec (2010) 'White Man Unburdened', *Financial Times*, 23–24 January.

'Sacked Holomisa Accuses Mbeki of Collusion' (1996) SA Press Association (SAPA), 1 August.

Sampson, Anthony (1999) *Mandela – The Authorised Biography*. London: HarperCollins.

Shain, Milton (ed.) (2006) *Opposing Voices – Liberalism and Opposition in South Africa*. Johannesburg: Jonathan Ball.

Sharansky, Natan (2004) *The Case for Democracy – The Power of Freedom to Overcome Tyranny & Terror*. New York: Public Affairs.

Slovo, Joe (1989) 'Has Socialism Failed?', http://www.marxists.org/subject/africa/slovo/1989/socialism-failed.htm.

South Africa Project, www.aryan-nation.org/Wake_Up_or_Die.pdf.

Sparks, Allister (2003) *Beyond the Miracle – Inside the New South Africa*. Johannesburg: Jonathan Ball.

Stengel, Richard (2010) *Mandela's Way – Lessons on Life, Love, and Courage*. New York: Crown Publishers.

Swart, Clayton (2013) 'Billions Flowed into South Africa Thanks to Mandela', *Business Day*, 9 December, http://www.bdlive.co.za/opinion/2013/12/09/billions-flowed-into-south-africa-thanks-to-mandela.

'The Death of the Rainbow Nation: Unmasking the ANC's Programme for Re-racialisation' (1998) Democratic Party discussion document, February.

Waldmeir, Patti (1997) *Anatomy of a Miracle – The End of Apartheid and the Birth of the New South Africa*. London: Viking.

Watson, Stephen (2010) *The Music in the Ice – On Writers, Writing & Other Things*. Johannesburg: Penguin.

*On the Contrary – Leading the Opposition in
a Democratic South Africa*

'Mr Leon's autobiography is eloquent, funny and rich … It is
an important record of South Africa's young democracy, witnessed
from the other side of the fence.' – *The Economist*

'The book seldom flags … The writing is far richer than in most
American or British political memoirs. It is also more frank.'
– ALEC RUSSELL, *Financial Times*

The Accidental Ambassador – From Parliament to Patagonia

'Witty repartee and fascinating stories … Leon is an excellent writer
and raconteur … eloquent and heartwarming.'
– SUE GRANT-MARSHALL, *Business Day*

'Intelligent, engaging and incredibly funny.'
– SHAUN SWINGLER, *Cape Times*

Lightning Source UK Ltd.
Milton Keynes UK
UKHW021000291121
394778UK00013B/1226